What Am I Doing Here?

A BEWILDERED AMERICAN IN BRITAIN

KATHY FLAKE

Lavender House Publishing
LONDON

Kathy Flake/Lavender House Publishing
London
UK
www.lavenderhousepublishing.com

What Am I Doing Here?/ Kathy Flake. —1st ed.
ISBN 978-0-615-98018-8

Contents

For Bailey, who for five years allowed me to see England through the eyes of a Golden Retriever.

"But the position of a foreigner with complete command of the same language has great advantages. I can take an objective view of England, which no Englishman can."

—GEORGE BERNARD SHAW

Author's Note

In January, 2005, I began writing about my life as an expat at my blog, unassumingly titled *What Do I Know?* (since there is nothing like moving to a foreign country to make you feel ignorant). I wrote about everything from food to politics to the wonderful adventures of my dog. What follows are some of my favorite posts, those most illustrative of my experiences here on this lovely island in the North Atlantic.

I've included the dates they were written, to avoid confusion over references like "George Bush" or "Tony Blair." I've made minor revisions from the original posts, again for clarity, and added a glossary. And forgive me, but I've used both American and British spelling and punctuation, where appropriate.

Introduction

I don't even like scones. So what am I doing living in the ground zero of scone consumption—the raisin-eschewing, currant-obsessed, Marmite-spreading island known as Britain?

I'm not quite sure how it happened. Ten years ago my husband suggested we move to England (something about a job he'd found in London) and I ignored him for seven months. Then August came round, and a moving van showed up at my house in Albuquerque, and five days later my possessions were all in large crates.

The dog, who'd never stayed overnight anywhere, was hovering, petrified, at the foot of the stairs when the last of the boxes was hauled out. Little did either of us know what lay on the other side of the Atlantic. I'm convinced if she'd known, she'd have bounced out of the house, tail wagging, eager to start her adventure. Off-lead walks, woods full of squirrels, a Common rich with the scent of deer, rivers shallow enough for a retriever to wade in, and sheep droppings for the taking...my dog found Heaven when we arrived here.

But as for me, well, woods full of squirrels—unwanted "American" gray squirrels, at that—were probably not the metaphor I expected. I guess I sort of assumed America, having been modeled on its Mother Country, had retained much of its technological proclivities, 220 current notwithstanding.

Everything was different here. I'd naively assumed like other poorly traveled Americans that the only differences between Brits and Americans was the way we refer to car parts: hood, bonnet, and so forth. I could handle that. And with two daughters well out of babyhood, I wasn't worried about any nappy/diaper mix-ups.

Oh, how ignorant I was. I found out right quick when the repairman asked where my "loft" was and I looked at him in shock, wondering how he'd mistaken my suburban house for a Manhattan apartment. A loft, it turns out, is British-speak for attic. So much for learning British lingo from Frances Hodgson Burnett. I was sure the Little Princess slept in the attic, but maybe I missed a nuance or two.

And that was only the beginning. I soon learned (or "learnt") any word with "er" was pronounced "ar" so that "derby" becomes "darby," yet Rs weren't pronounced at all. Learned academics say "pwabably" all the time, a phonetic foible which would have American parents phoning the speech therapist.

I also quickly learned that confrontations were frowned upon. Mustn't ask a server (as waiters are known) for the whereabouts of a delayed meal; they'll just politely tell you to bugger off (by refusing to make eye contact, a skill Brits excel at). It all made me rather "cross," a word that's incapable of conveying the depths of my good old American, war-mongering, fast-food fueled ire. I felt like The Ugly American whenever I raised my voice, my bland Nowhere, USA accent sticking out like a Fourth of July firework.

Through the years here we've celebrated many Fourths of July, prepared quiet Thanksgiving meals, bought Mother's Day cards in March, and remembered not to call the repairman on Bank Holidays and Boxing Day.

I've become adept at driving on the wrong side of the road, weave through double roundabouts like a figure skater, and skid to a stop at zebras. I remember to call an eggplant an aubergine and a zucchini a courgette. I add extra vowels to words and delete prepositions from my sentences and when I'm feeling assimilative I even ignore hardwired lessons of subject-verb agreement and talk about the government as if there are several of them.

I haven't yet figured out the appeal of scones, or of *Little Britain*, but the British Isles have become my favorite spot on earth.

I mean favourite, of course.

—Kathy Flake
March, 2014

CHAPTER ONE

I May Have Some Trouble Adjusting

In which I experience culture clash, and find a few things I don't like. Am I an Ugly American? Or just a misfit?

January 23, 2005

Holes

NOT LONG AFTER MOVING IN, I had to have a talk with our estate agent (known by the less extravagant term "real estate agent" back in frugal America). After discovering our gas bill was through the roof, my husband went poking round (a very British thing to do) and it turned out the gas really was going through the roof. Seems our fireplace has no damper. On a clear day (well, one day last month), you can see blue sky at the other end of the flue.

Not only that, but there's a deplorable lack of weather stripping, and as for attic insulation, let's just say I've seen Barbie dolls dressed more warmly.

We remedied the situation as best we could, by affixing cardboard under the flue, and sadly foregoing the pleasure of a roaring gas fire. Then I called the estate agent (who is also the property manager) to complain (a very American thing to do) and I learned that gaping holes in one's house are perfectly acceptable. In fact, "It's against the law to damper a gas fireplace," she told me. "Otherwise people might gas themselves and not even know it."

"Oh, they'd know it all right," I replied, but American snark is lost on the Brits. "What about weather stripping?"

"That's unsightly. None of the posh houses have weather stripping." (Posh, for you Americans, is a term meaning "expensive, in an overwrought way." It can also mean "ugly.")

Furthermore, I was told, "Insulation isn't the landlord's responsibility."

Greenhouse gas, apparently, isn't either.

Since Brits are presumed to be too dense to know how to open a damper, or install a heat-activated one, I had a feeling I knew the answer to my next question: "And why aren't there electrical outlets in the bathrooms?"

"People might electrocute themselves."

Us Americans, it seems, are somewhat smarter than the average Brit, or perhaps we are indeed dying in unprecedented numbers, in our bathrooms, blow dryer in hand, one foot in the tub, and a roaring gas fire in the hearth.

"You'll just have to get used to the way we do things here," the agent told me, with a definite ring of glee in her voice.

Foolhardy American that I am, I adopted an equally tart tone and ended the conversation: "Well, until you're willing to talk about weather stripping, Kyoto is off the table!"

(There are times when it's handy to have a lunatic, warmongering, earth-ravaging President. We've considered ending arguments with recalcitrant servers and parking attendants by taunting "Oh yeah? Well, your Prime Minister's our President's poodle!")

Okay, we might not be smarter than the Brits, but at least we don't have gaping holes in our houses.

We, of course, prefer them in our ozone.

January 26, 2005

Nanny State, Part II

I HEARD ON THE RADIO this morning that the Department of Culture, Media and Sport want to reduce the size of the Teddy bears given away at fairs, in order to avoid enticing children into gambling. Well, it's about time! I personally know hundreds of gambling-addicted children. Some, sadly, have taken to selling drugs to afford another round of baseballs to toss at the plastic ducks, in hopes of scoring another giant Teddy bear.

Don't get me wrong. I think a primary role of government is to protect its citizens. But this, coming from a government that allows those citizens to drive on the WRONG side of the road?

I smell disingenuity. (It smells a bit like baby's nappies.)

And while I'm at it, how about the Department of Culture, Media and Sport try enforcing a speed limit or two? Many's the time I've been happily driving along, at a sedate pace of 60 mph, when a car whizzes by at 90, the driver shaking a fist at me for daring to drive the speed limit on a single carriageway.

Don't even try a dual carriageway, unless you're trained in Formula One racing and have a fully paid up life insurance policy.

So where's that nanny state when you need them? Wrestling Teddy bears from children, and trying to keep us from electrocuting ourselves in the tub, that's where.

January 27, 2005

Nanny State, Part III

THIS MORNING I WAS listening on the car radio to a discussion about the government's swimming guidelines. Apparently parents can't be trusted to keep their children safe in the pool, so the Health and Safety Executive issues handy guidelines. Lifeguards use them to prevent a single mother from entering a pool with two children, since she's clearly exceeding the limits of safe supervision.

As I listened, chuckling at the sometimes silly extremes of the nanny state, I drove past a parked school bus. Yes, that's what I said: I drove PAST a school bus, loading children. There are no rules here about stopping for school buses. No red stop sign swinging out, insisting you STOP! (In fact, stop signs are rare in Britain. Instead you'll encounter the well-bred "Give Way" or the baffling triangle painted on the road.)

What I want to know is, what kind of nanny state prevents parents from teaching more than one child to swim at the same time, yet allows its nation of speed demons to fly right past a school bus?

But then, the nuances of British driving still elude me. For weeks, I thought this sign meant "no picnic tables (i.e. rest area) ahead:"

The sign indicating a motorway looks like a picnic table.

And imagine trying to decipher this at breakneck speed:

Roundabout and roundabout and roundabout again?

Yes, your nanny state allows you to drive through five roundabouts, one after another, yet you cannot take five children to a swimming pool. (Children being much harder to keep track of than your way round roundabouts, apparently.)

At least there's an A&E (Accident & Emergency) conveniently located at that last roundabout. Clearly the nanny state is on top of some things.

Now if they would just properly warn us when there are no rest areas ahead. You never know when you might want a nice cuppa tea and a sitdown.

February 2, 2005

Litterbugs, Repent!

ACCORDING TO THE NEWS, London is getting filthier:

> *London managed to score only 43 points out of 100 for cleanliness, compared to the east of England, the most pristine place to live with a scored of 72.*

But the rest of England is getting cleaner: "For the first time in years, a national survey has shown improvements in the state of England," Alan Woods, chief executive of "Keep Britain Tidy" said in a statement.

I'm not surprised to read London is getting filthier, but the rest of England getting cleaner? They must be living on a different island (perhaps Rockall Island, population 0).

The island I live on—approximately the size of Pennsylvania, population 60 million—is a litterbug's lair. There's an appalling amount of trash strewn about the highways, streets, and pavements (sidewalks) of once-fair Britannia. On a two-mile stretch of the A40, enough litter has accumulated to fill a good-sized lorry or two. Plastic bags wave jauntily from the trees, orange peels wait for decomposition along the sidewalks, crisp wrappers remind me constantly I'm not in Kansas anymore. (I never was, actually, but I bet it's cleaner than the Home Counties.)

I've seen unmentionable rubbish on the way to the train station, where commuters park along the street and hurry to catch a train.

Dirty nappies, discarded baby bottles, sandwich packets—sometimes complete with a sandwich, to the dog's delight.

Maybe it sounds better when called "rubbish" instead of trash, but it's still disgusting. I've heard that during the Troubles, rubbish bins were removed after IRA terrorists used them to hide bombs. People became accustomed to tossing trash on the pavement.

The Troubles are over. And the only Irishman I've seen in my neighborhood is a Wolfhound, who doesn't look like he could be bothered to detonate a blast.

Even worse than litter, which can at least be overlooked, is graffiti, which shouts to be noticed. On the way to Oxford I saw scrawled on an embankment "Thank God For Jesus Christ," to which someone had added "Amen!" Defacing public property, no matter the degree of one's religious fervor, is just tacky. (In the old days of Oxford, such messy fanaticism would have been rewarded with burning at stake.)

I think the problem is there's no teary-eyed Native American icon to prod the national conscience. Perhaps William the Conqueror could be enlisted to come back, wave his sword around a bit, and shame the Tesco-shopping descendants of the once-proud Angles and Saxons into cleaning up their act.

If not, I'd consider bringing back the stocks.

April 11, 2005

British Elections: The Issues

I'M FINALLY GETTING A HANDLE on the issues in the British Parliamentary races. On the Beeb (which is how the locals affectionately refer to the BBC) the other day, I heard Michael Howard promise to crack down on yobs. I still haven't figured out what a yob is, but it has something to do with people who toss eggs and perform other unsociable acts, which earns them an Asbo—Anti-Social Behavior Order. Politicians are keen on stopping yobs, since other types of crime haven't really caught on here.

Then I got a flyer from my local Conservative council candidate. He's addressing the vitally important issue of flytipping. Again, I don't have a proper handle on what flytipping is, but it has something to do with rubbish, since the dustmen are the ones to call if you see flytipping going on.

I've got my eyes peeled, for yobs and flytippers.

July 7, 2005

London Pride

(Author's note: On 7 July, four London locations were bombed by terrorists.)

I LOVE BRITAIN. I didn't just discover that today, when suddenly my country is under attack. (Yes, lately I've been thinking of this beautiful island as "my" country. You'd claim it too, this time of year.)

I said to someone just the other day, at some point I forgot how "weird" things were here and accepted it as normal. Roundabouts, pubs with funny names, "neighbours" who spell funny, a government that thinks it's Mary Poppins, the whole bit.

But today my neighbours weathered a storm with grace, grit, and a bit of an in-your-face attitude they may have learned from their American cousins.

All is normal, despite bomb blasts on tubes and buses. The FTSE barely trembled. Trains are running again and The Archers is on the radio. Take that, Al Qaeda, or whoever your sorry asses are.

Londoners are a tough breed. I was at the Imperial War Museum a few weeks ago, where I read about the Blitz that killed 41,000 Londoners. They sent their children away, stiffened their resolve, buried their dead and removed their rubble to Regent's Park.

I saw a man interviewed today. He was calm, despite having blood running down his face. He told his story, then walked away.

His mum and dad probably lived through the Blitz. They'd be proud of him now.

I learned something else today: London Pride isn't just the name of a beer. It's a song by Noel Coward, who certainly was no coward.

London Pride has been handed down to us.

London Pride is a flower that's free.

London Pride means our own dear town to us,

And our pride it for ever will be.

...

In our city darkened now, street and square and crescent,

We can feel our living past in our shadowed present,

Ghosts beside our starlit Thames who lived and loved and died

Keep throughout the ages

London Pride.

July 9, 2005

In London Today, We Laughed

I RODE THE TUBE in London today. We walked past Edgware Station, cordoned off now, flowers stacked nearby. The TV station Al Arabiya had a camera crew there, and one of their celebrity anchors was shaking hands with admiring bystanders.

In the instant on the platform as the train braked to a stop, I had to decide which carriage to step into. I chose the one with blonde women. When a man got off later, I glanced at the spot where he'd been sitting, in case he'd left a bomb.

After a couple of stops, I forgot about being scared. Millions of Londoners must have felt the same way yesterday when they went to work.

In Covent Garden, we saw *The Producers*. Gaiety ruled. Who knew Hitler could sing and dance?

On the way home, a man got on the train with his little girl. He was showing her the Tube map (Londoners teach their kids the Tube map the way we used to teach ours the state capitals) and she said, That's the purple one the bomb was on. No, no, he said. Don't say that word. She said it again. Incident, he said. Call it an incident. But he was laughing. We all were.

Then we got off, and in the lift was a photo of a missing person. John Downey, who didn't come home that night. And there were more flowers, outside Edgware.

September 26, 2005

The Old Bailey: For Fans of Bloodsport

TODAY I WENT TO the Old Bailey (no, not in handcuffs) and viewed two murder trials. It was much more entertaining than sitting around listening to The Bloody Archers, and in fact, I may have become a court junkie. I do not understand the national fascination with cricket when there are far more entertaining matches to see, for free at that.

The Old Bailey is also known as Central Criminal Court, and is the primary criminal court in the United Kingdom. Anybody who's anybody will be tried here, including Jeffrey Archer (no relation to the Archers of Radio 4 fame), the criminal author—err, crime fiction author.

One trial today featured a young woman, who may or may not have killed a man who may or may not have been her lover. The other involved a man (named Ozzy Osbourne, in honor of his idol—I am not making this up!) who may or may not have bragged about killing a man—or not. (Vagueness intentional. Libel laws are tough here, and I do not want to end up in Old Bailey wearing leg irons instead of khakis.)

Knives are the murder weapon of choice here. If you live with someone who sometimes flies into rages, best not to keep a set of Chicago Cutlery around.

Some other things I noticed: The barristers really do wear wigs. They look totally ridiculous, and the stupid things are obviously itchy (one poor QC kept scratching, or maybe he was feigning puzzlement). They are best left on the nags from whence they came. (They cost about as much as a decent horse, too.)

The barristers, or QCs, are really sharp, and call each other "my learned friend" which makes them all sound very posh. Think Perry Mason meets Dumbledore. In a wig.

Don't waste your money on a "private tour," which turned out to be a fifteen minute briefing beforehand and directions to the visitors' entrance. You get in for free, and once you're inside a tour guide can't talk to you anyway. But go ahead, pay five quid for someone to show you which door to enter if you need the reassurance.

However, Barbara, the security guard, was able to talk to us, and she was most helpful. I think she deserves the five pounds we paid to the other guy, but I hear she prefers chocolate.

Old Bailey stands on the site of Newgate Prison, one of the most notorious hellholes in the world. Public hangings occurred here regularly. Then someone invented football, and bloodsport was never the same.

October 2, 2005

Going Native

EXACTLY ONE YEAR AGO this morning, I arrived, bleary eyed and jetlagged, at Gatwick Airport. When I got to the car park, I woke up immediately. The cars all had steering wheels on the wrong side, and when the driver pulled away, I realized he was driving on the left side of the road. Somehow, I imagined they only did that for the movies.

As we drove up the M23, tiny cars and vans flying past, I told myself I'd never, ever drive here. Though I'd never been intimidated by a gas pedal before, with all new road markings and road rules, I no longer felt so surefooted.

I still laugh when I think about that, every time I race to Gatwick to pick up guests.

Driving on the "wrong" side of the road is just one of many oddities I've gotten used to over the past year. In fact, they no longer seem odd. Maybe I've been assimilated.

I no longer find it strange to hear "schedule" pronounced "shed-ule" nor do I cringe at the odd subject-verb agreement ("the company are"); in fact, I do it myself. My spelling has evolved into a form of "Britlish." I pronounce "Birmingham" and "Cheltenham" without mentioning pork products, and I even go on about "hurricuns." (Though I no longer experience them—hurricanes are far too violent to be tolerated here.)

I love to hear the multi-flavoured accents: the Northumberland Geordie, the hefty Scottish brogue, the hodge-podge mid-country cadences, the proper Londonese, the posh public school intonations. I find myself dropping my own R's—car becomes "cah" and perfect is "puhfect."

BBC Radio 4 is my constant companion, tickling my fancy in a way NPR never did. In fact, I'm thinking of naming my next pet "Cromarty" after the Shipping Forecast. In the morning, I listen to the medley of stirring British anthems on BBC radio. My heartbeat quickens to "Rule Brittania," slows to "Greensleeves." (I haven't started humming Oasis tunes in the shower. Yet.)

We won't discuss The Archers. Everyone is allowed one mistake.

Somewhere along the way, I've fallen in love with England (Wales, Ireland and eventually Scotland too). Just like a love affair, it's hard to say exactly what aspect is most pleasing—is it the green hills? The history encroaching on a thin modern veneer? The orgasmic flowers? The cute little Minis, the iPod of the car world?

Living here is a lesson in history. I've literally tripped over it, on steps indented by the trampling of feet over thousands of years. Serendipitous connecting-the-dots occurs often: One night I was reading a book about Charles Lamb, the English essayist, which mentioned a street in London I'd just been walking down that afternoon.

Even the dirt, after centuries of absorbing Man and his excrement, reeks with a history all its own.

Not all is roses, either the "Peace" kind or the War of. Commerce, for instance, is not as simple here as in the States, involving numerous trips to different shops in order to buy a newspaper, a book, and a light bulb. And don't even get me started on light bulbs: there are so many different types—bayonet, screw, narrow, wide, golf ball, candle—that you must carry one around in your pocket in order to identify the exact replacement.

The British are remarkably patient. (The ones in a hurry all emigrated to Australia, I think, thus leaving the genetically placid.) I'm always the one standing in the queue, looking pointedly at my watch, or the impatient American harrying the waiter: "Do you realize (real-

ise) we've been here an HOUR? I could get faster service in France!"
(That gets their chèvre every time.)

And while we're on the subject, I've a few other complaints: The
dodgy décor (I don't care if you watched the last coronation on that
sofa, it's rubbish!); the outdated plumbing (what's so difficult about
single-handle faucets?) and have I mentioned the drafts lately?

But most of the time I'm happy to muddle through like a native,
light bulbs in my pocket. I make my way through the *Rough Guide to
England* page by page, determined to see it all while I'm here. Other
expats say they felt the same way their first year, afraid there's not
enough time to see it all—in a place where the last thousand years are
scattered around like litter on the A40.

So I rack up the miles, century by century, and wonder how people in America manage, driving on the wrong side of the road as they
do. Plus, what could there possibly be to see in a country that's only
existed a couple hundred years?

August 5, 2006

The Story of How I Don't Exist

THE OTHER DAY I TOLD my local bank manager that British banking laws were stupid. You should have seen how big his eyes got; I don't think people normally confront him with reality like that.

Even though I've been here almost two years I don't have a bank account. My husband does, but as I wasn't around when he opened it he couldn't open a joint account. You have to appear in person, with a briefcase full of documents, all with your actual name, current address and incarceration history on them, in order to have your name appear anywhere on a bank account.

It hasn't been too much of a problem, but then someone gave me a cheque. I first tried to cash it at the bank it was drawn on; no luck. You'd think I was trying to hold up the institution, asking for my money like that! Then I tried to deposit it in my husband's account, with him at my side. Still no luck. Again, you'd think I was trying to get away with robbery or something, depositing money INTO a bank! Who ever heard of such?

So then we went over and sat in front of the bank manager, who looked like someone out of Mary Poppins. My husband explained how he wanted to put me, his lawfully wedded wife, on his account. The bank manager listed the sorts of documents, all of which would have to be recent, that would be acceptable as proof of my identity and residence. I didn't have any of them. My name's not on the utility bills either, and our rental agreement is over three months old—yep, turns out I don't really exist.

The bank manager was apologetic, but I was having none of it. "Your banking laws are stupid," I told him, "and also they suck eggs."

He looked embarrassed, but not nearly distressed enough. I suspect he's never even seen Mary Poppins.

My husband tried to broker peace: "They just have really safe banks," he said, "and they want to keep them that way."

I rejected his efforts: "And banks in the States AREN'T safe?" Plus we both remembered the last time he'd stopped at the bank on his way home: it was closed due to an "incident" that had occurred at the neighboring bank. ("Incidents" here always involve police and a certain amount of British understatement.)

Pig twaddle, I told the bank manager, and my husband too, who by this time was earning my ire by not immediately bashing in someone's head. What's the point of being a rash American if you can't go all Pulp Fiction on someone?

I ripped up my useless cheque in a dramatic show of pique, then stormed out of the bank, hoping I'd run into Samuel L. Jackson on my way out. No such luck, not even Dick Van Dyke dancing on the rooftops.

I've calmed down a bit now, but as long as I don't exist I've decided I'll break some laws. No more speed limits for me! Parking wardens can kiss my bumper! I'm running amuck and taking no prisoners.

That bank manager will rue the day.

December 18, 2006

Signs, Signs, Everywhere Signs

I SAW A SIGN at the entrance to the woods the other day, and when I got close to read it, it said something like "don't come over here, we're trying to grow wildflowers in this spot."

And today I saw another sign, which is far easier to read:

By the way, Americans might find this custom quaint: when British people leave notices out for people saying things like "Please don't park here" or "Please pick up after your dog" they always preface it with the words "Polite Notice."

Such a contrast to the "Recycle or Die!" sign I saw when I first visited Madison, Wisconsin.

April 20, 2009

This Must Be Discouraged

THIS SIGN AT THE POND reads, in typical polite British-speak: "Kindly refrain from feeding the ducks. This food has caused a rat problem. This must be discouraged."

My dog understands why we mustn't encourage rats, but she sure liked it when people tossed bread out for the ducks. She fondly remembers many good tidbits scavenged in this location.

One would imagine the ducks aren't too happy about this development either.

I'm thinking of posting my own sign: "Pick up your litter, you tosser!" Maybe I haven't quite got the hand of this polite signage yet.

September 6, 2010

Six Years Later: An Expat Looks Back

SIX YEARS AGO TODAY, the first wave of the Flake family arrived on the shores of modern Great Britain. Daughter Number Two and her dad arrived first, followed a week later by Daughter Number One, and then, on the second of October, I arrived with the dog, who managed to get through the defenses set up by Defra*.

I look back at those days with amusement. While being driven up the M23 from Gatwick, I swore I'd never drive here—not only were the cars and trucks (which turned out to be lorries) all going the wrong way, but the road markings made no sense. A month later, I got behind the wheel of my car and managed just fine.

Driving isn't the only skill I've acquired. I've learned a second language, too: British-speak. I now know that people can be "pressurized" and women have "the mee-nopause" which has something to do with "ee-strogen." I know that commas don't behave properly over here—they can turn up, literally, anywhere, in a sentence (or not) and spelling is often accomplished by adding some silent vowels here and there. I try not to say the word "garage" if I can avoid it, since I always pronounce it the French way, but on the other hand I buy aubergines and courgettes.

I am very keen on aubergines. I am brilliant at maths, since "brilliant" here simply means "pretty good." And I violate trademark law every time I hoover my carpet.

If I ask a shop "clark," not clerk, for corn, I am directed to the chicken feed. "Berkshire" is pronounced "Barkshire." Likewise "Hertfordshire" is "Hartfordshir." Fortunately I will not go to jail for mispronouncing "gaol" or "Nike" or "Adidas."

I have learned to ask for "water," not "wadder," and I even specify plain, not sparkling. My daughter is at "uni," not college, since she's already graduated from high school. I buy a "return" ticket or a "single," but never a "single return," clearly an oxymoron. I cannot bring myself to speak of collective nouns in the plural, however, so my government are not doing anything about the economic situation. Which, by the way, is referred to on these shores as the "credit crunch" rather than a recession.

I am learning new things all the time. Recently, I learned that a "stremmer" is a weedwacker—not nearly as descriptive. Prepositions are still surprising me: I've run across the construction "bored of" twice in the last 24 hours. The letter "R" is elusive, even in the highest elocutionary circles: Bwitish people should pwactice saying it more often, especially if they're being interviewed on the wadio. (I should offer to trade my R's for their T's.)

The lessons go beyond language, of course. There are subtle behavioral differences between our two cultures. Losing one's temper in public is not done, which makes me very angry. (See "The Story of How I Don't Exist"; that was not well done of me.) Complaining about poor service is considered improper (not rude, nor mean, since one means vulgar and the other means cheap), which makes me lose my temper. In the face of adversity, one must pretend as if nothing is wrong, especially if the adversity is medical. Extra points if you can explain away the cast on your arm with a cheery, self-deprecating tale, preferably involving the phrase "pear-shaped."

On the other hand, complaining about the weather is encouraged. (Unless, of course, you're in Malaga, then you should be getting pissed—no, not a violation of the first rule above, but rather falling-down drunk.)

Not all is English cheer, or rather "cheers!" I've discovered the dark underbelly of the English psyche, which the Irish, Scots and Welsh surely were on to long ago. Now it's the Eastern Europeans and Asians who are unwanted here, and the baldness of the anti-immigration rhetoric surprises even me: I've been told all of the problems here began when they let in "those foreigners."

Foreigners like me, I suppose, since there is also a streak of anti-Americanism here, usually on display in the *Daily Mail*. If I read one more article about how Americanisms like "24/7" or "have a nice day" are destroying the social fabric of England, I think I'll lose my temper. In public.

As an expat, I am aware that the minute I open my mouth, I am immediately identified as a North American. I try not to let down the home team.

I admit, however, to feeling a certain amount of schadenfreude when my home team managed to hold England to a 1-1 draw in (or is it "at"?) the World Cup.

That's football, not soccer. Played at Wembley—yes, Wembley, really—with a W. I drive past there quite often, and the road markings couldn't be clearer.

*Defra: the government agency that handles quarantine and the new Pet Passport Scheme.

January 2, 2012

The Hazards of Living in a Nanny State

NOT LONG AFTER I moved here I noted the many contradictions of living in a supposed "nanny state," a term used to describe the sometimes extreme measures taken by the government to keep its citizens safe and healthy.

For instance, I heard about a town that cut down all its lime trees because a limb had fallen, and it was feared that the trees could fall on unsuspecting passersby. Graveyards are also seen as places of potential fatal hazards after an old leaning tombstone fell on a child once, thus requiring notices to be put up. And then there's the size of Teddy bears: mustn't encourage our tots to gamble at the Fun Fair by offering too-large bears as prizes!

But anyone who's ever called Great Britain a nanny state obviously never endured a night of anything-goes fireworks. The three weeks of pyrotechnic frenzy around Bonfire Night sound like Baghdad during Shock and Awe. BOOM! Welcome to Buckinghamshire during Diwali.

Recently, a friend on Twitter mentioned that New Jersey didn't allow any fireworks at all for home use. I was surprised to hear New Jersey was even more health and safety conscious than the UK, with its Teddy-limiting laws. New Jersey? Isn't this the birthplace of concrete shoes?

Yet the law in the UK seems to allow celebratory fireworks year round. A few months ago, my daughter took the dog on a walk and came home with a strange story about some twenty or so weird glowing apparatuses she'd seen in the sky. Since she had a friend along for confirmation, we believed her, and it wasn't until an American neighbor put on a Fourth of July fireworks show in his garden that I realized what she must have seen: Chinese lanterns. Apparently it's entirely legal to send flaming bamboo and paper balloons into the atmosphere. As we watched our Chinese lanterns disappear over the M25, I wondered if there were any thatched cottages nearby.

Surely these must be safe, I reminded myself—I live in a nanny state! I'm not even allowed a damper in my gas fireplace, or an electrical outlet in my bathroom! No worries. Right?

But today I read in my local paper that over New Year's, two fires were caused by Chinese lanterns. A car caught on fire when one lodged underneath, and a tree went up in flames after one was caught in its branches.

I found this comment interesting:

Chris Bailey, head of Buckinghamshire Fire & Rescue Service's community safety team, said: "You can't control the direction they take or where they will land."

He warned that unsuitable locations for flying lanterns included "areas near telephone and power lines, areas near standing crops, anywhere near buildings with thatched roofs, areas of dense woodland and areas of heath or bracken."

Which pretty much describes all of England.

A nanny state that can't be bothered to regulate dangerous fireworks, yet doesn't allow dampers on gas fireplaces, in case citizens kill themselves? It's one of those contradictions that make me more certain than ever that political labels are meaningless. I live in a theocracy, where the state media broadcast church services, yet much of the population never attends church or even thinks about religion very often.

It would be enough to make my head explode, except for the fact that I'm sure the Health and Safety Executive has issued a guideline against exploding heads.

So bring on the nanny state. I'd like more of it, please—just don't tell me how big my Teddy bear can be.

CHAPTER TWO

Language Barriers

If you come to England thinking you'll have an easy time of it since you speak the language, think again.

April 18, 2005

All Your Lampshades are Belong to Us

I ORDERED SOME NEW LAMPS the other day, and when they arrived, I realized the Brits aren't the only ones who don't speak fluent American English. Here's the "Assembling Instruction For K/D Lamp Shade:"

Step 1: Open the box and move out the lamp shade.

Step 2: Disperse the white ribbon of the shade, then Hold the metal round tache up.

Step 3: On the side of the shade you will see several metal nogs Which enwrapped with shade cloth, insert the up side of the nog into the small hole where there is a direction arrow

Step 4: After finish inserting all the nogs one by one, Push them back next to the shade.

Step 5: The K/D lamp shade be finished by Successfully assembled according to the above four steps.

Yeah, right.

This reminds me of something I heard on Radio 4: The government are pressurizing maths teachers to give more ticks to their students who sat their exams.

Huh?

November 15, 2005

Scoring Points for the Home Team

YESTERDAY IN MY History of London class I realized I was once again fulfilling the role of class clown. (Mind you, I was never a very good class clown, but it was better than being the class smarty pants.) As the other American was absent, it fell to me to represent the Yank view. (I even had someone corner me for the answer to a crossword.)

The instructor said something about Dr. Johnson, "who I'm sure needs no introduction," he added. I glanced around, and no one else was looking puzzled. Not wanting to be the class idiot, I kept my mouth shut. Later the instructor casually mentioned that Dr. Johnson wrote the first dictionary. My eyebrow shot up, and he continued, with a decided twinkle in his eye, "but the Americans think Noah Webster did."

Huh! (Not the first time he's tried to put one over on us. There was that crazy story about Pocahontas earlier—haven't these guys watched Disney?) I raised my hand and took one on the chin for the mother country. "Actually," I said with a wide smirk, "I'm pretty sure Noah Webster did. That's what I was taught in school."

The instructor, a kindly old chap, laughed. "Yes, that's what they teach the Americans." He then went on to tell us that the two men were in sort of a race, and your view of who won apparently depends on how you pronounce the word "schedule."

Later on, I was able to regain the moral high ground. When he reminded us that Gray's Inn was spelled with an "a" instead of an "e," I did my eyebrow-raising routine again. "But isn't that right?" I asked, prepared to defend my newfangled American spelling.

That's when he said that it was us Americans who had the right of it. Around 1880 a group of people got together and decided to change the spelling, he told us. Clearly, the Americans use the proper old spellings of words. (Could I possibly have smirked any louder?)

I then helpfully suggested we start a movement to put right the spelling, and everyone chuckled, finding my enthusiasm amusing. Right. I was serious, though. I'm getting tired of not being able to spell properly in any language. I'm starting to toss in the odd "u" here and there, just in case.

I've had previous tiffs over language with my "neighbours." When the small local rag ran a series of letters to the editor that poured scorn on the "Americanization" of the language (they're particularly peeved with the expression 24/7) I reminded them their own contributions to the language were no more brilliant: i.e., using "brilliant" to describe some minor mental exertion (such as making an appointment), and "hoovering" which is clearly a trademark infringement. "Lovely" has also been downgraded, particularly by shopworkers to convey approval for handing over payment.

I place the blame squarely on Will Shakespeare. Teaching us that language was fluid—what was he thinking?

As for that Webster/Johnson controversy, I'm pretty sure whichever guy won, Webster at least got the spelling right.

October 4, 2006

Learning About Cider the Hard Way

IT'S CIDER SEASON for those of us in the Northern Hemisphere. On our walk today someone thought they smelled apple pie baking—it was the windfall apples that no one's bothered to pick up. That's what I call an optimistic nose.

It got me in the mood for cider, though—real, American apple cider.

Here's a warning: Cider in England means something entirely different from delicious, crisp American apple cider. It's hard cider, of course, and it's obviously an acquired taste. I found this out the hard way, when my friend and I bought small cups of freshly brewed hot cider at Borough Market last fall. Anticipating a proper taste of tart New England, we took a sip, then grimaced at each other over our cups. We stepped behind the stall and discreetly poured it out.

Hard cider is awful cold; hot, it's like drinking fresh piss.

The Royal Standard of England, which claims to be the oldest public house (pub) in England, serves a pear cider—perry—that looks as clear and sparkling as champagne. I haven't tasted it—I'm still reeling from my Borough Market experience—but a friend who did approves. I'll take her word for it.

Did you know we have the Norman Conquest to thank for apples in England? Now Normandy is known for its Calvados—apple brandy, which is a far better use for apples than hard cider.

I also learned via Radio 4 today that lager has surpassed stout as the most popular beer in England, mainly due to marketing. Apparently you are more sexy if you drink lager.

Cider, however, needs more than marketing to make it sexy. I've smelled rotten apples that were more appealing, frankly.

February 25, 2007

Babel, Baybel, Read Your Bible

THE OTHER DAY ON THE NEWS they were talking about Microsoft's patent abuse. Except they weren't talking about "patents" they were discussing "pay-tents."

It turns out long vowels are more popular here than short vowels (or wee vowels, as they have in Scotland). I've also learned the British have a problem with too much "mee-thane" instead of "methane" and women have something called "ee-strogen" and when that runs out they go through "the mee-nopause."

It makes you understand what Moses was talking about in Genesis:

> 7 *"Come, let Us go down and there confuse their language, that they may not understand one another's speech."*
>
> 8 *So the lord scattered them abroad from there over the face of the whole earth; and they stopped building the city.*
>
> 9 *Therefore its name was called Babel, because there the lord confused the language of the whole earth; and from there the lord scattered them abroad over the face of the whole earth (Genesis 11).*

Which is why tonight you may need a pronunciation guide to the Oscars, depending on which side of the Atlantic you're watching from.

The movie Baybel is popular over here, but the movie Babel may win the Oscar over there.

July 30, 2007

Lessons in Language at the Fun Fair

THE FUN FAIR CAME TO TOWN last week, which meant the dog was bugging me to go. I'd taken her last year. Using my prodigious human skills I won her a stuffed unicorn, which she carried home. She also likes the candy floss (don't get excited; that's just Brit-speak for "cotton candy") and burgers that invariably end up on the ground at these events.

So when we saw it had arrived, she was all like "Take me to the fun fair, Mom!" which she conveyed by tugging on her lead as we walked past on the main street. I can't resist a tug on the lead, so we went over and sniffed around.

I didn't have any money, but fortunately the fun fair wasn't open yet. The scents were plentiful, however.

Two little boys, about four years old, approached us, children of the workers who live in the caravans parked behind the fair. One, clearly the official spokesman, told me his friend Billy was afraid of dogs, since they'd been known to eat people. Billy had been watching too much BBC, I told him, and explained that my dog preferred eating Pero dog food to people.

Then he asked me if my dog engaged in something called "diggoes."

"What?" I asked, not sure I'd heard him properly.

"Does she diggoes?" he asked again, and after I'd asked him to repeat himself one more time, I got it: "No, she doesn't dig holes except when she helps me garden."

That cleared that up.

It reminded me of the time soon after I'd moved to London. We were walking in Paddington Green Park (one of the loveliest spots in London) and a gentleman with a trembling whippet approached. "Zattagewl?" he asked.

I peered at him in confusion. "What?"

"Zattagewl?" he asked again, and then again. I was about to explain to him that I didn't speak the language, but fortunately I deciphered his words: "Yes, she's a girl," I said, and he was much relieved. Seemed the whippet only liked girl dogs. Or gewl dogs, rather.

Oddly, even though the man spoke with the most upper of upper-crust accents, similar to the Queen's, and the little boy was dropping his h's in a decided working class manner, neither one made sense to my American ears.

It's much easier to understand my dog.

January 10, 2008

Separate, with an R

IN CLASS TODAY I had another American moment, as I'm starting to call these little mental disconnects when my lack of Britishness causes me to say something stupid.

Last time, I was scribbling notes furiously as the instructor pointed to a slide of the dome of St Paul's and explained that the dome rested on an inverted "salsa."

"A salsa?" I said. "How do you spell that?"

"Salsa," he replied. "A salsa. S-a-u-c-e-r."

"Oh, a saucer!" I exclaimed, pronouncing it correctly, with an R on the end. It was not, after all, some new architectural term I was unfamiliar with; it was merely the quaint British custom of neglecting to pronounce the 18th letter of the alphabet.

Then today, I was nodding off while we talked more about churches in London, specifically the ones built by Hawkesmoor after the New Churches in London Act of 1711. The instructor explained that while the original act called for building 50 churches, only about twelve were actually built, due to the fact they ran out of money.

It occurred to me, just exactly who was "they"? So I asked, and the answer woke me up. The government was paying for the churches to be built, with the help of a coal tax. A century later, they proposed to build 100 new churches, but again ran short of funds.

"That blows my mind!" I blurted, then, a little quieter, added, "I guess it's the American in me."

This time, no one laughed.

I spent the rest of the class pondering this, despite a tantalizing discussion of the finer points of St Mary Woolnoth church.

It seems to me, your views on the separation of church and state are pretty much dependent on whether or not you pronounce the letter R.

December 4, 2008

In Total Darkness, I Stiffen My Lip

I'M BACK. You probably didn't know I was gone, did you? But for several hours this afternoon and evening I was without power, which means I was without internet. Prophetically, I'd just updated my Facebook status: "Kathy is leaving the internet to fend for itself for a while" I wrote, around 3 p.m.

A minute later, everything shut down. No lights, no BBC buzzing in the other room, no Radio 4 on the radio upstairs I always forget to turn off, no lights.

No computer. No internet.

I knew immediately what had happened. For several days now, the water company has been tearing up my street, attempting to fix sewer lines for the residents downstream. The workers had accidentally cut the electricity lines to my house.

In England, it is very rare to lose power, unless you live on the coast and you're experiencing gales. Here it just doesn't happen. My neighbor, of the sewer line mess, told us it had happened only four times in thirty years.

Regardless, when I phoned the power company, I got a royal runaround. First, you have to determine which power company services your area—not at all that clear. Then you have to find a number, without aid of the internet. Then you have to wait on hold for a long time, attached to a phone cord since the cordless won't work—and light is fast fading. But if you try to call an 0800 number from your mobile, you're charged.

Then when they finally answered, I got another runaround, had to call another power company—Southern Electric for future reference—and then had to convince the live person on the other end that I actually had a problem. They told me to go to the "customer box" and flip a switch to determine that it wasn't a problem within the house, since they hadn't received any other calls.

Of course I had no idea what a "customer box" was. Turns out it's the fuse box, which is in my garage—but the garage door wouldn't open without electricity, right? Unless I could find a key to the side door, with the help of my weak torch light.

See what I mean? This doesn't happen very often here.

Finally I convinced them it wasn't my fuses, and that the workers digging and jackhammering outside were at risk unless they GET SOMEONE IMMEDIATELY OUT HERE TO FIX THIS! It helps to have an American voice sometimes. They were probably frightened I'd sue for damages—Americans are known here as being frightfully litigious.

Meanwhile, conscious of the rapidly approaching dark, I lit candles and found torches and batteries. I pondered the possibility of starvation and freezing to death. Once I'd done all I could to stave off either, I found I was in dire possibility of dying of boredom.

I cleaned my house in the dim light (wouldn't want anyone to find dirty countertops when they pick up my body!), and as the light finally gave out, I ate pistachios and cleaned out the bookmarks on my laptop. I phoned my sweet little 80-year-old neighbor, to update her on the arrival of Southern Electric, and she told me I was doing a "champion job" surviving in the dark. She lived through the Blitz and knows a champion job when she sees it.

My husband came home and we opened a bottle of wine, admired each other in the candlelight, and pondered litigation.

Then the lights flickered back on, and things were suddenly normal again. I had a gazillion emails—turns out the world had continued on as we took a short break from the modern world of electricity and internet. I was high on lavender scented candles and Bordeaux by this point, and all thoughts of litigation had fled.

I can handle anything, I am convinced. Bring on the Blitz.

November 29, 2010

In Defense of America and Its Isms

"Why can't they use British English which we all understand, instead of American slang which in my view spoils otherwise interesting articles?"

THIS IS GETTING ROUTINE. Yet another newspaper article on those dang Americanisms! This time in *The Guardian*, not known for its defense (defence?) of America on any issue, yet now oddly mounting a tepid defense of so-called Americanisms it's allowed to creep into its copy.

I've been here six years, and I've never had a Brit insult me to my face. Yet every few weeks I read another insulting tirade against my language. Faceless Americanisms are a favorite target of letter-to-editor writers, most of whom I imagine as slightly creepy old men ranting about "kids these days" (except they'd never use the word kid unless talking about a young goat). "Mojo" seems particularly offensive, ironically. Likewise "brownstone," a term used almost exclusively in New York City. Someone from the American South would never live in a brownstone, but they'd happily "duke it out" over their right to use the term. As for "lickety split," well, I don't think I've heard that one used since I was a wee lass.

Oops. Pardon that Scottishism.

I'm convinced these rants against our version of English is simply a socially acceptable, non-confrontational way to express one's dislike of the United States and its inhabitants in general. I don't hear rants about Germanisms, only the word "kindergarten," which they attribute to our side. I don't hear rants about Frenchisms, indeed, I'm forced to order courgette and aubergine rather than zucchini (an Italianism) and eggplant.

And don't even get me started on idiotic Britishisms (I'm surprised they haven't changed the expression "hoover the floor" into "dyson the floor"). Yet my countrymen back in America have no problem with their media's embrace of Britishisms. I've never read a letter complaining about cute British expressions like "arsehole" or "gobsmacked." And "snogging" seems to be pretty popular on both continents.

No, Americans aren't threatened by encroachment to their language. Only to their borders—but then that's another topic. (I'm really tempted to suggest that those Brits offended by "ugly and unnecessary Americanisms" ought to be subjected to a TSA screening.) We weren't once the world's greatest military power, with colonies spread on four different continents, now reduced to losing at the World Cup (the sport Americans, by the way, refuse to refer to as football). But perhaps that's just schadenfreude.

Oops.

I find all this defense of British English—an amalgam of Anglo-Saxon and Norman French—tiresome, and when I'm feeling particularly prickly, downright insulting. Read the comments on any such article, and then dare to reply "Natch!" instead of "Naturally!" One reader wants to "open up on your ass" for speaking such slang. (I think he meant "pop a cap on your ass.") Really? Our American slang makes you feel murderous? Hmmm...I can't say I've ever felt the same emotion reading the word "nappy" in reference to diapers, but then I don't typically feel road rage toward lorries, either.

Maybe it's because the Scots and the Irish and even the Welsh are finally taking back their languages from the English and their Anglo-

Saxonisms. That leaves little territory for proper British English these days. Do the math...err, maths.

Apparently British English has lost its mojo. It's high time they woke up and smelled the dark roast Americano. Or maybe they should just step up to the plate. Whatever!

Meanwhile, I'll defend to the death my right to "vacuum" my floors instead of "hoover" them. And I might have to: Britain, remember, has no right to free speech. A man has been prosecuted for something he dashed off on Twitter—will the use of Americanisms one day become a capital offense? That would really suck...err, I meant to say, I wouldn't be too keen on that.

Oh, and have a nice day!

April 5, 2013

Boilers, Garages, and Torches

YESTERDAY I WOKE UP to a cold house. Not that unusual, since I get up before the heat kicks on at 5:30, but by 5:45 I noticed the radiator still wasn't growing warm. I put it down to the time change, but later my husband investigated and discovered the boiler was out.

I only had a vague idea what a boiler was, but I knew it was a bad thing when they went out. I'm still not up on where they go when they "go out" but I've heard horror stories about what happens when they do, especially if it's over a holiday. And it wasn't just a simple matter of relighting the pilot light (which would be something I'd call in an expert for, frankly) but the thing was really, truly, "out."

It meant that the water that flows through the radiators wasn't being heated by the boiler, which is apparently its job. The boiler is equal to a furnace in the States, then. Without one, the house doesn't have heat.

The house was already starting to chill. I called the aptly named Frost (our estate agent, which is like a real estate agent), who sent a plumber out to discover what the problem was.

That's right; a plumber, not an HVAC specialist, which is what would happen in the US. Because the boiler uses water, it's a plumbing problem.

Fortunately the plumber isn't an ordinary Joe Plumber; this guy is really good at what he does. He's identified plumbing problems before and fixed them, after other plumbers were stumped. It's almost enough to make me take back every bad thing I've said about British plumbing. Almost.

He got to work and made some calls, wrote down some part numbers, and identified two parts that needed to be replaced. But there were other problems with the old boiler, which caused it to exhaust carbon monoxide to the outside vent. As soon as he said the word "carbon monoxide" I swooned. Not really, but I did stop listening, and apparently the landlord did too, or else saw lawsuits in his future, so the plumber was quickly given the go ahead to replace the whole thing with a newer, energy efficient model.

Except not so quickly after all. Not-Joe the plumber will have to re-route the pipes from the laundry room to the garage, where the new boiler will reside. It will be Tuesday or Wednesday before the thing is up and running. Meanwhile, he's loaned us two space heaters.

And that's not all: The hot water heater, which runs from the same boiler, has an electric immersion backup, which blew up when the plumber tried to turn it on, creating a shock in the tank—fortunately, the fuse box did what it was supposed to do and averted disaster, though not a nasty scare when we heard the "pop!" After our discussion about carbon monoxide I was in swooning mode again, frankly.

Fortunately, Not-Joe the Plumber was able to find a new electrical immersion element and replace the old one, which was corroded and twisted. He seemed to think that was awesome, and even took a photo, so I did too.

Here's the thing: I'm always a bit nervous when repairmen come to the house. It's hard enough for me to convey what's wrong with some gadget or another, not knowing the least thing about boilers and toilets and other residential mechanical ailments. But add to that my ignorance of the language, and I hesitate to say anything. The first time anyone came here to fix something he asked to see the "loft." "We don't have a loft," I replied, wondering if he'd mixed our property up with a chic London flat. He was incredulous, since clearly, we had an attic. It took both of us a few minutes to realize we weren't simply ignorant; we were speaking two different languages.

Even after all these years, yesterday I stupidly offered the plumber a flashlight. I quickly backtracked and offered him a "torch" instead. Which still strikes me as a bit ludicrous. A torch was the last thing I wanted to light, with possible gas leaks about the place.

And then there's my reluctance to say the word "garage," the source of most things mechanical, including the "consumer unit." (That's a fuse box, for those of us who prefer a more descriptive English.) The word "garage" has a funny pronunciation here, as if someone who hated the French tried to pronounce it in the least French way they could, so it comes out "gair-ridge." That's just a sound that's fundamentally difficult for my American tongue to wrap round.

So I ended up handing the garage door opener to the guy, pointing in the direction of the "gaRADGE," and telling him to open the "door." The word door is easily understood by anyone, I've found.

Since I'll be spending three days with Not-Joe next week, I'll have to brush up on my British English and figure out new ways to avoid saying "garage." Maybe from now on I can call it the "boiler room."

In the meantime, I'm rethinking that torch idea. Some old fashioned fire would feel good just about now, but if I want to light my fireplace I'll have to call the gas service man, and who knows how that conversation would turn out.

September 11, 2013

Blinded By Language

I WENT TO THE OPTOMETRIST yesterday, since I'd noticed my glasses weren't working as well as they should. I have a "complex prescription" as they say here, which means that the diopters of correction, including myopia and astigmatism, are equal to or greater than ten.

Needless to say, I go several times a year to the eye doctor, for either glasses or contact prescription updates and purchases. Yesterday, as I sat in the chair reading the eye chart, I struggled as usual to see the tiny lines on the bottom. At one point the eye doctor, a new one I hadn't seen before, corrected me: "Zed."

Oh. The Z was a "zed" not a "zee." Or an H either, as I'd mistakenly thought it was. And no, an "H" is not an "aitch," it's a "haitch," at least in Southern England. (I've been told up north they refer to it as the Americans do, an "aitch," but I haven't traveled much up there. Or rather, travelled.)

That's when I realized that I'd been misreading the chart all along, all these nine years I've been living in Britain, subconsciously absorbing the local English dialect. I can usually manage to get "lorry" right, or "boot" or "garden" (instead of "yard") but I'd not been mindful of the letters, probably because I don't attend first grade (or "year one") at the local grammar school.

I do hear the announcer on the Bakerloo line reminding people to "alight here for Zed S L" which stands for the Zoological Society of London. (It has a funny name because it was founded in 1826, before zoos were called zoos.) And I silently chuckle when people say "haitch" as if they're in a Victorian drama. I remember to call it a "zeb-ra" crossing instead of a "zee-bra" crossing, maybe because that actually makes more sense phonetically. And there's a famous map book of London called "London A-to-Zed" that's been replaced by map apps now.

So I finished my eye exam, remembering to use "zed," but I couldn't bring myself to say "haitch." My life here is a series of phonetic compromises: I say "to-mah-to" but not "shedule." I use periods instead of "full-stops" and place them either in front of or outside of the punctuation, as I see fit.

It turns out my eyes have gotten slightly better, at least one eye has, while the other is worse. But with correction I can see 6/6, not 20/20 (meters, instead of feet). And I need something called "occupational" glasses, a combination of computer glasses and reading glasses. But not even the most up-to-date prescription will make that Zee look like a Zed to me.

CHAPTER THREE

Driving

Once I learned to drive on the left, I discovered a whole new side of England, where the grass really is greener.

August 23, 2005

The Electric Acid Road Test

MY DAUGHTER AND I went to Reading today, which reminds me a lot of Ireland. Even with a map you still drive around in circles, dead lost.

People in the States can't understand what it's like driving here. Driving on the other side of the road is the least of it; you soon adjust to that. It's that there are so darn many roads, with roundabouts every few feet forcing you to decide which spoke to get off on. "Three o'clock or nine?" I shout and my daughter looks confused. "It's only eleven thirty," she tells me, at which point I'm already on the way to Basingstoke.

Of course when you need a roundabout in order to make a U-turn, that's when the road turns into a dual carriageway and you whiz by your destination, the largest—and most elusive—mall this side of London, The Oracle. (Oracle, my ass! If that place could read my mind it would move to the suburbs of Basingstoke which is where any self-respecting mall should be located. It's about convenience, people! Get a freaking clue!)

At one point I turned into the bike lane, which totally embarrassed my daughter, until I told her it was perfectly acceptable to drive in the bike lane here. I was lying, but what does she know?

I refuse to resort to GPS. I tried spellcheck, and now I can't spell for crap. I don't want to lose my sense of direction the same way. Besides, I don't even think a sat nav could figure out Reading.

We did accomplish our goal, though, which was to find Tom Wolfe's Electric Acid Kool-Aid Jungle Juice Test, or something like that. She needs to read it for her American History class, which makes me wonder just which part of American History they'll be learning this year.

I'd also wanted to go to the Museum of Rural English Life, which is inexplicably located in downtown Reading, but the only road that went there was going in the opposite direction, and I couldn't convince my daughter driving the wrong way on a one-way was perfectly acceptable too.

Maybe after she reads Tom Wolfe she'll be ready for more adventures in Reading, but first I'm getting a psychedelic bus. Hey, who needs GPS when you've got LSD?

July 29, 2006

Dorset: Geology, Anthropology, and Animal Intervention, All on One Coast!

The Dorset coastline

YESTERDAY I TOOK THE GIRLS to Dorset, a journey that should have been accomplished in around two hours, but took almost four instead due to the traffic on the M3. We crawled between Winchester and Southampton (about 10 miles) for over an hour and a half, slowed by the enormous number of people who decided that yesterday, predicted to be the last of our current heat wave, was the perfect day to go to the beach.

I estimate there are approximately 30 million people living in southern England, and at least half of them were heading to

S'hmpton (motorway shorthand) yesterday between 9:30 and 11:00. (Note to my Scottish readers: This would have been an excellent time to launch an invasion. Payback for Culloden and all that other nasty stuff, you know?)

Our destination was Monkey World, which actually has more apes than monkeys, but let's not get too picky with terminology. The only apes I did not like were the human ones. There were far too many of them. Have I mentioned there are approximately 30 million humans living in southern England? The half that weren't at the beach were at Monkey World. The crowds, though, were actually a good thing, since the entrance fees go to support more primate rescues.

Monkey World is where the Animal Planet hit show *Monkey Business* is filmed. It's really an Ape Rescue Centre, and their mission is to rescue abused and exploited primates from around the world. The television show is like *Hollyoaks* for primates, filled with drama and melodrama. Typical storyline: chimpanzee Cherry neglects her baby; keeper Jeremy must take little Pip away and hand raise her. Will her mother ever accept her again? Meanwhile, Jim and Alison Cronin are in Thailand, searching for abused orangs. They find them at a tourist trap, learning to ride bicycles. It's heartbreaking, and entertaining, just like *Hollyoaks* (a nighttime soap opera, for you Americans).

From Monkey World it's only a short drive to Lulworth Cove on the Dorset coast. This section of coast is known as the Jurassic Coast and is a haven for fossil hunters. We stayed on the beaten paths, so we didn't see any fossils, but I did get called a "stupid American twat" by some guy who was beating his dog. I don't know what it is about me that I can't keep my mouth shut when I see an animal being abused. Since the dog in question had returned, with a big smile on her face, when the stupid British prick had called her, I was especially shocked when he started hitting her with the lead. I tried to explain that punishing a dog for obeying didn't make any sense, but you can't really argue with a guy who uses words like "twat." I'm sure his girlfriend was impressed by all that manliness. I hope she gets treated better than the dog.

But anyway, Lulworth Cove was a geologically fascinating place, or so I've read. Since my knowledge of geology is pretty much limited to identifying flat rocks for rock skipping, I just enjoyed the scenery. We heeded the warning signs and stayed off the rocks, but some teenagers were jumping into the water from atop the rocks. My anthropological observation: the apes at Monkey World were much more evolved.

A couple of miles away is the potterishly named Durdle Door, which I suspect has been around much longer than Harry Potter. Again, I'm no geologist, but imagine a few dozen millennia in fast motion, eroding away the limestone to create such an image. For movie trivia buffs, the opening sequence of *Pirates of the Caribbean* was filmed here, as well as the Tears for Fears video for "Shout."

There were beaches at both Lulworth Cove and Durdle Door, the former, especially, filled with inappropriately dressed humans. (I would insert a lecture here on what people over sixty ought to put on their bodies, and that should include sunscreen and not bikinis, but hey, who'd listen to a stupid American twat anyway?)

I will offer this advice: if you're in search of a relatively uncrowded beach in southern England, head to Durdle Door. The two beaches on either side of the Door were relatively human-free. Although personally, I'd head across the Atlantic to Florida if I were in search of a beach, which I'm not—there is just way too much sun at beaches, and with my complexion, sunshine is a deadly toxin.

For some reason beaches here are covered with gravel instead of sand. It must have something to do with geology, but it makes for uncomfortable beach lounging. A few truckloads of play sand would take care of that problem, but then what do I know? I'm a stupid American twat who prefers to lounge on beaches fully clothed.

We didn't have time to stop in the little village of West Lulworth, but it was filled with thatched stone cottages. They were the cutest things I saw yesterday, other than the baby chimps.

The Dorset coast is approximately 130 miles from London, if you ever care to visit. You really should, although don't attempt this on a hot sunny day; otherwise you'll compete with half of southern England for space on the M3 as well as the beach. Your best bet might be to take a train to Poole or B'rnmth and hire a car from there.

Or better yet, stay longer. The coastline is constantly changing—well, every millennia or two.

July 8, 2007

Signs of the Apocalypse?

YOU SEE THE STRANGEST THINGS while driving down the road in Dorset.

No, this isn't a reaction to the attempted bombings last weekend. It's at a military camp near the coast. And yes, a few minutes later we heard loud booms. Very loud booms.

What with the stinging nettle and the sudden gunfire, the bucolic English countryside can sometimes offer some nasty surprises.

August 20, 2007

First, Ditch Your Sat Nav

ONE OF THE THINGS that's so cool about England (and all of Europe, for all I know) is that you'll be driving around, minding your own business, and then you'll come upon something totally stupendous. Like this fourteenth-century abbey, located on the grounds of a boys' school, that looks like it belongs in a Harry Potter film.

The front of the abbey, with a tiny car for size comparison.

The abbey was never finished, but somehow survived total destruction during the Dissolution. It now serves as the chapel for the school.

Nearby was the village of Milton Abbas, which lacks the crowded, ramshackle appearance of most English villages.

Milton Abbas, one thatched cottage after another.

This is due to the fact that it was a planned village, created after the owner of the Abbey tore down all the houses in the original village, flooded it to make a lake, and relocated everyone to this community planned by the landscape architect Capability Brown.

It's scenes like these that are why I insist on getting off the main roads as often as possible, and why I always bring along a copy of *The Rough Guide to England* everywhere I go. And why I still use a map instead of a sat nav. Because our GPS device has no idea that I'd rather see thatched cottages instead of service stations along my route.

September 12, 2008

Britain to join 20th Century?

THAT'S RIGHT; THE GOVERNMENT HAVE finally proposed to introduce bus service to its primary (elementary) schools. A year long report has concluded what any parent in America could tell you: putting your kids on a bus is better than driving them to school. It's safer, uses less gas, and gives parents more flexibility to do fun things like have careers.

It will come as a shock to most Americans, as it did to me when I first moved here, but British schools don't offer bus service at the primary level (years 1 through 6, or up to age 11). This means parents are slaves to the school bell. The "school run" is the time between 8:30 to 9:30, and in the afternoon, from around 3 to 4, when parents must pick up their children from school, either by car or on foot. Local traffic is crazy during this time.

To make it even more complicated, some younger children are released 15 minutes before older children, requiring parents to wait if they've more than one child.

Also, you can't simply drive up and drop off your children, as happens in the US. You must park and walk your child to the front door, and do the same in the afternoon.

My friends with children in British schools are very limited, having to race to school in the afternoon in order to be standing outside when the bell rings. Most moms I know don't work. With no after-school programs, there's little alternative other than child minders or nannies. (The American school here, which most older American children attend, does offer bus service for all ages.)

So it's no wonder that on the radio the other day, they were talking about why women haven't risen to senior positions in their careers. I screamed at the radio: "School buses, people! What's so complicated about that?"

Apparently a lot. But if the recommendation is followed, that may change—although it will come at a cost. The report says that most parents will pay £1 or £2 a day for the service, unless they're on the free lunch program.

It will radically change the school run, eliminating it for people who live more than a mile from school. It will also radically change my life: There's a primary school in my neighborhood, and traffic is a nightmare every morning and afternoon during the school year, effectively turning a busy two-lane road into a one-lane obstacle course. Walking traffic, too, clogs up the sidewalks—I avoid walking the dog during the time the sidewalks are filled with pushchairs and children and moms with mobiles on their ears.

Little by little, Britain seems to be catching up to last century's social and technological innovations. What's next, free wifi in cities?

August 4, 2011

Free Recovery, Await Rescue

NOT LONG AFTER I MOVED HERE, I noticed a motorway sign at the entrance to a stretch of roadworks (i.e., a construction zone). "Free Recovery, Await Rescue" it said, and I immediately envisioned a damsel in distress, awaiting a handsome knight in shining armor at the side of the road. I didn't know then that "recovery" was the British term for "tow" but the sign has always been a delightful reminder to me that I live in the land of knights and damsels and other medieval bygones. (Let's just leave our feminist sensibilities at the door for a moment and go with this, shall we?)

Until yesterday, the only time I've needed rescuing on an English roadside was after a hard winter when the back roads were a series of enormous potholes. My tyre (why Americans refuse to use this quaint spelling remains a mystery) had a "puncture," as the British call a "flat" in their typical understated way. I left a message on my handsome knight's mobile, and my knight—err, husband—soon arrived on his equally handsome steed—err, red motorbike, and replaced the torn tyre with the spare. (No, I can't change a tire. Or a tyre. We're going with this, remember?)

Yesterday I was racing down the A3 in the fast lane when I felt my car wobble as if I'd hit a rough patch. But the rough patch was my tyre coming apart. I managed to control the car, hop over three lanes and then my luck kicked in. Normally an A-road has only a limited shoulder, but there was a blue P—my second favorite sign in England, for Parking. A lay-by, exactly where I needed it! (A lay-by is a pulloff on a main road, where sometimes sandwiches and flowers are sold, and is long enough to park a few vehicles. It's where you pull off when you heed a "Tiredness Kills. Take a Break." sign.)

I pulled in, stopped the car and turned on the hazard lights. With shaking hands I reached in my purse, pulled out my mobile and punched in my knight's phone number. The phone flashed a low battery warning (my least favorite sign) and cut itself off.

Uh oh. "What the hell kind of damsel doesn't charge her Virgin mobile before leaving her castle?" I asked myself as I took stock of my increasingly bleak situation.

I was on my way to Haslemere in Surrey for a dog training seminar, and if I didn't show up no one would pay much attention. My husband assumed I'd be there all day, and didn't expect me home until evening. Even if I could have called RAC, our roadside assistance service, we'd let the service lapse in May, as we contemplated moving this summer.

I opened the boot of my estate car (translation: I opened the cargo door of my station wagon) and searched for the spare. Maybe I could haul it out and look helpless. I didn't see the spare (where do they hide those things, anyway?) but I did see a warning triangle, mandatory in every EU vehicle. Mine was folded up into a space-saving shape. I attempted to unfold it, but it was fashioned like one of those three-dimensional puzzles you sometimes see at Amish farmhouses. Opening one was beyond the skill level of the average damsel, much less a technically disinclined one. I decided I didn't want to look too competent—no one would stop, and by this time I had my hopes pinned on a knight of the realm, or at least someone who knew how to change a tyre.

Stuffing the triangle and my panic back into the boot, I closed the door and gazed at the oncoming traffic. If I saw a police vehicle, I'd start waving my arms. Sure enough, soon a van came up with police markings. I waved furiously, then watched as he sped past the lay-by.

Maybe he'll call in for backup, or circle around, I thought, but just before I turned around to face the traffic again, I noticed a recovery vehicle—a flat-bed tow truck—pull into the end of the lay-by. As he backed up to my car, I felt giddy with relief, enchanted by the sight of the rescue I'd awaited a mere five minutes for. (Isn't England great? Shortest damsel rescue time in the EU.)

A middle-aged man got out of the truck and my first impulse was to hug him. I smiled wide and offered him cash instead, thinking he could fix my flat and I'd be on my way. He gave me an indulgent smile, as if he knew he was talking to an idiot. "You won't have the proper tools," he said, and I believed him. I'd seen what was left of my tyre—a few bits of rubber clinging to the rim. Even I knew that the rim could be damaged from a high speed blowout.

Within five minutes, my knight in a shining tow truck had pulled my car onto his truck, and I hopped into the passenger seat. I decided the music he was listening to at top volume wasn't so bad. He asked where I was going and I shouted over the music, "Haslemere—it's a few miles off the A3." He was heading to Southampton, and was happy to take me to a tyre repair shop in Haslemere, provided we could find one.

A half hour later, after we'd stopped two pedestrians to inquire about a tyre shop, we pulled into Chessington Tyres. A youngster roughly the same age as a page in King Arthur's court helped my middle-aged knight remove my car, and I realized my fairy tale would end happily after all.

I even made it to the seminar on time, although I was a sweaty and blistered damsel by the time I'd walked there from the tyre store. My knight had disappeared—I'd hoped to catch his name so I could recommend him for an OBE in Her Majesty's honours list.

I'm sure he had other damsels, as well as the odd German tourist, to rescue on that hot day.

There's a moral to my tale: Damsels, keep your mobiles charged, and keep your RAC dues paid. Always have enough cash on hand to pay your knight. (Turns out £60 is the going rate for recovery these days.) And handsome knights married to witless damsels should listen when his wife comments on the condition of the tyres, and possibly even give her a lesson in how to change a spare.

CHAPTER FOUR

History Lessons

During my time here I've taken several history and archaeology courses, where I was often the only American. Which put me at a disadvantage: Americans don't come equipped with the ingrained knowledge of history Europeans do, having trod upon the land where much of our documented human history occurred. I tried not to embarrass myself, yet sadly, it happened more than once.

March 1, 2005

Stonehenge: Astronomical Observatory, Or Christo's Muse?

THE GATES, the artist Christo's latest project that's currently showing in New York's Central Park, seems a bit, well, derivative. Some early humans over in Britain had the idea first, only they used 45 ton boulders instead of orange sheets. (Modern art is so wimpy!)

This seems as good a time as any to write about my visit to Stonehenge on New Year's Eve. Not exactly the Winter Solstice, but we did ensure we arrived in plenty of time to avoid the fall of darkness, which hits southern England around 4:30 in mid-winter. A steady wind on the Salisbury Plain wrapped the cold around us and reminded us we were at 51 degrees latitude, further north than Moose Jaw, Saskatchewan.

A rather ordinary highway, the A303, plows through bucolic English countryside toward Stonehenge. Suddenly the monolithic stones appear, rising off the Plain like ancient city skyscrapers. This city, though, is guarded by sheep and friendly English Heritage gatekeepers. We paid our fee and later traded up for an English Heritage membership, a sound investment that quickly paid for itself.

Many myths surround Stonehenge. Most people assume the stones were placed by Druids as a worship site. But the stones were in place 2000 years before the Druids ever got around to dancing sky clad under the full moon.

So who were the early humans who built this "theme park" out in the middle of the woods? (Although the Plain is cleared of forest now, in ancient times the surrounding area was heavily wooded.) Just who carried these stones, weighing as much as 45 tons, from as far away as Wales?

The best guess seems to be that the Stonehenge site was begun by the people of the late Neolithic period (around 3000 BC) and carried forward by people from a new economy which was arising at this time. These "new" people, called Beaker Folk because of their use of pottery drinking vessels, began to use metal implements and to live in a more communal fashion than their ancestors. Some think that they may have been immigrants from the continent, but that contention is not supported by archaeological evidence. It's more likely that they were indigenous people doing the same old things in new ways.

Stonehenge was built in three stages, starting in around 3000 BC until around 1500 BC. First it consisted of circular earthworks, where perhaps tribal meetings took place, or where ancient deities were worshiped—or both. Its alignment even then suggested a relationship with the midsummer sunrise.

The stones were added later, beginning in around 2500 BC, when the four-ton bluestones were likely transported by rafts from the coast of Wales. The bluestones were arranged in a horseshoe pattern, and later were rearranged (in perhaps the earliest example of feng shui).

Two or three hundred years later, the heavy sarsen stones, some weighing as much as 45 tons, were carried overland—and uphill—from the Marlborough Downs, 20 miles to the northeast. Humans did the work themselves, not contracting the job out to oxen or horses, using ropes and sledges. It's estimated as many as 500 men were needed just to move the stones, with another 100 to arrange the timbers used as rollers underneath. These were laid in a circular pattern outside the bluestones, inside pits dug with antler picks. Heavy lintels were then placed atop each pair of sarsens. To lift the lintels the construction workers probably erected a "crib" of timber frames, and constantly levered the lintel ever higher while raising the framing until it was equal to the height of the sarsens.

The lintels were locked in place using mortise and tenon joints, carved into the stone with stone hammers. The outside surface of the lintels were cleverly shaped to form a continuous circle. These refinements set Stonehenge apart from the other stone circles found in Europe. (Let's see Christo copy THAT, using only antler picks and rock hammers!)

Significantly, or not, the axis of the sarsen circle points toward where the sun would rise on the longest day of the year. Over the centuries, the stones were rearranged to adjust for the variation of the midsummer sun. This suggests the stone circle was some sort of astronomical observatory, or perhaps even a mere calendar—an important tool for an agrarian society.

Why go to this much trouble? Perhaps one day the future inhabitants of earth will say the same thing while looking at archaeological evidence of the Twin Towers, or Westminster Abbey. Since no one left a written record, or even got round to inventing writing (imagine!), the purpose of the site will remain speculation. (Until, that is, someone gets round to inventing time travel.)

Over the centuries, many of the stones have disappeared, used as building materials or destroyed. In the nineteenth century an enterprising blacksmith in nearby Amesbury rented hammers to tourists hoping to capture souvenirs. The land was deeded to the government in 1918. What remains today is a remnant of what must have been truly awe inspiring, a monument to human achievement, regardless of its original purpose.

Stonehenge is not as commercialized as I'd feared, but it could use its own museum, or at least an interpretive center. Currently, only a gift shop and a small snackbar muck up the atmosphere. A free handheld audio set is provided, which gives you a running commentary as you walk around the path that circumnavigates the stones. (Inner circle access is available by prior arrangement, during the hours the monument is closed to the public.)

And if you aren't yet sufficiently impressed by what ancient peoples could accomplish, without so much as an HP calculator or an accurate watch, then head ten miles down the road to Salisbury Cathedral, a magnificent structure built in 1258, and be sure to see the original copy of the Magna Carta displayed in the Chapter House.

You can also see Europe's oldest working clock at the cathedral—which, being so near the world's oldest calendar, somehow seems appropriate.

Note: Since this was written English Heritage has added a proper interpretive centre to the site. It only took a few thousand years, but finally visitors to Stonehenge can have an experience worthy of the effort it took to build the stones in the first place.

November 25, 2005

Battle of Blenheim, as Told by Charles Spencer

WEDNESDAY NIGHT I WENT to see Earl Spencer (Di's brother) give a lecture on the Battle of Blenheim. He's written a book, *Blenheim: Battle for Europe*, which stars his ancestor, John Churchill, the Duke of Marlborough.

When I first came to London, I noticed the name Blenheim everywhere: Blenheim Gardens, Blenheim Crescent, and so on. (Thirteen Blenheim-named streets, according to London A-Zed.) I'd never before heard of Blenheim, which is interesting in itself.

We've all heard of Waterloo, and now the Battle of Trafalgar (especially this year, the 200th anniversary) but the Battle of Blenheim gets short shrift in the history books. That's a shame, since if not for the exploits of John Churchill and his sidekick Prince Eugene, there's a pretty good chance we'd all be speaking French.

Occasionally throughout history, the forces of good manage to ally against the forces of evil, in this instance Louis, the Sun King. He thought he should be emperor of Europe, and what's more, that all Europe should be Catholic, which worried the Protestants no end.

His ego was matched by the size of his army (roughly the size of the US army today). He broke treaty after treaty and was determined to carve up Spain for himself.

The man had to be stopped and it was up to John Churchill to do it. With unexpected cunning Churchill raced his troops 250 miles, surprised the French in Germany, and decisively defeated an army that hadn't been beaten in 60 years. What's more, he treated his troops well, seeing that they were well fed and looked after—a novelty at the time.

As Earl Spencer pointed out, history is interesting because of the people involved, not the battles and the places they fought for. John Churchill, who was made the Duke of Marlborough and given the land and funds to build Blenheim Palace, sounds like a decent chap, especially when held up to the often barbaric standards of the time. He was also handsome, and true to his wife Sarah, which doesn't hurt in a hero.

I can't wait for the movie.

January 17, 2006

A Norman By Any Other Name

TODAY IN CLASS I learned that the nomenclature of history is dependent on who tells the story. In the case of the Vikings, it was their victims, the literate Christian monks, who told the brutal tale we know today.

No word on if they used the term "terrorist."

Those same Vikings married slim French women and changed their name to Norman, which used to be pronounced Northmanni. Guys named Norm are forever grateful; they could have been named Rollo after the first Viko-Norman duke. (Who was given the title after signing a treaty with King Charles the Simple, who wins the Worst Name in the World contest hands down.) Instead, Rollo gave his name to Rolo Caramels, for which dentists everywhere are grateful.

January 24, 2006

History in Your Back Yard!

The dog discovers an ancient artifact at the nearby hill fort.

I'VE MENTIONED THIS BEFORE, but the thing I love most about this place is how it's just dripping with history. Really, you can hardly walk a mile in England without stumbling upon some archaeological ruin. There's a reason for that.

Today in my Norman class we learned that by the time of the first Viking incursions, around 800 AD, most of the usable land was already taken. Imagine, a property shortage already! Those Anglo-Saxon property investors sure must have made a killing when the Vikings came, wanting semi-detached houses with three reception areas and an ensuite. And a garden just the right size to bury their hordes of danegeld. (Nowadays, of course, it takes a horde of dane-geld just to buy a property here.)

On Sunday we walked to the Iron Age hill fort I'd heard about. Even though it's hardly a mile from my house, I'd never ventured there before. Sounds silly, but there are dozens of archaeologically worthy sites within an hour's drive, so I haven't even got round to the nearer ones.

But it was a lovely day for a walk to a multivallate hill fort, so we took the dog and risked our necks crossing the A40. People from America imagine anything old must be heavily guarded, with steep admission and surrounded by a cyclone fence, but like most archaeological sites here, this one has nothing more than a sign directing you to pick up after your dog.

It's sort of a local dog hangout, with 26 acres of mostly open land surrounded by earthen ramparts you'd almost miss if you didn't know they were there. The area has been excavated twice, but yielded little in the way of artifacts. That's why they think it must have been occupied only during times of danger. "Terror alert Orange! Proceed to the hill fort! Bring bottled water and duct tape."

The most interesting sights now are the huge old oak trees, probably planted in the seventeenth century, that surround the area. They vie with the ones in Sherwood Forest that I saw recently for size and scruffiness. One has a brick "chimney" built within, though it's recently crumbled. A slab with the date "1900" was lying on the ground nearby, indicating the bricks were erected at the end of Victoria's reign.

Surrounding the hill fort are posh houses on a private road, their gardens backing up to the double ramparts. Imagine having 2000 years of history, right in your back yard.

February 7, 2006

A Tale (or Two) of Two Kings

APPARENTLY MILITARY PROPAGANDA did not start in the twentieth century. Today in history class we read contemporary accounts of the Battle of Hastings, written by the eleventh century version of embedded reporters. The Norman accounts talked about the "the most valiant duke" William, aka the "most noble conqueror and hereditary lord" to whom "our written tribute cannot do enough justice."

Of course that doesn't stop them from trying.

The Norman accounts are careful to vilify the fratricidal Harold, who after swearing fealty to William double-crosses him by crowning himself King of England when everyone knew William was the rightful king, having been promised the crown by King Edward, his boyhood pal.

William really had no choice but to invade England, now did he? Blessed with divine inspiration and much prudence, he managed to hastily put together a fleet of "3000 ships," rather than the 300 most later historians attribute to the Norman duke, proving that military exaggeration is nothing new either.

We are told William did have one momentary lapse of prudence: he put on his hauberk back to front, but he good naturedly laughed this off, and did not see it as an ill omen, as any less divine ruler naturally would've.

Norman public affairs officers insist that William, after having conquered England, thoughtfully avoided despoiling the land as well as the womenfolk. No mention is made of the vast stretches of land later listed as "waste" in the Domesday Book. Sometimes war is not pretty, they say.

The English chroniclers, on the other hand, had nothing but nice things to say about King Harold, "a noble earl who all the time had loyally followed his lord's commands" and who reluctantly accepted the throne after Edward's death. May God have mercy on his soul. (And not a word from anyone about Edward's sexual preferences. Hmmm...)

Harold then valiantly overcame invaders to the north, including his brother Tostig, who'd gathered support from the King of Norway, whom Harold was also forced to kill. (God is not asked to have mercy on their souls.) Harold graciously allowed their sons to return to Norway, and to this day Norwegians think twice about picking fights with the English.

Unfortunately, Halley's Comet chose this moment to appear, and the "star with hair" was seen as an ill omen.

We all know what happened next, and not even the most sympathetic embeds could whitewash the bloody battlefield of Hastings. Harold, God have mercy on his soul, met his end, some say with an arrow in the eye.

In the English chroniclers' version William is no gentle ruler. Despite his promise to be a gracious lord, William allowed his soldiers to "ravage all that they overran." He was crowned king at Westminster, and then promptly "laid taxes on his people very severely."

Not much has changed since 1066. Our chroniclers today are just as eager to tell the stories the victor wants told. One day historians will attempt to sort it all out, but the record will be muddied: soil inevitably clings to those embedded in battlefields.

March 14, 2006

Blame It on Rome

I LEARNED A COUPLE of things in my Norman class today, but I learned one the hard way.

Every class period I end up asking a stupid American question, but I try to limit myself to one. This time, it was a real doozey, a subtract-100-points-from-the-SAT, what-were-you-doing-in-World-History-class question. When the instructor said that Matilda, William the C.'s granddaughter, had married the Holy Roman Emperor, I waved my hand, determined not to let this 900-year-old scandal go unremarked. Since when could the pope marry, I asked, a stupefied expression on my face.

Which quickly turned to horror, that same feeling you get when you dream you're in class naked. The Holy Roman Emperor is "neither holy nor Roman," the instructor corrected me, in his ever-so-gentle way, nor is the Holy Roman Emperor even a man of the cloth, and thus is allowed, even encouraged, to enjoy conjugal bliss.

Well, color me duh! It turns out the Holy Roman Emperor ruled what is now known as Germany. Who knew? Not me, that's for sure, though the rest of the class seemed to have received a memo on this earlier.

Then later we were talking about the friction between the rulers of England and the Church, which did not begin with Henry VIII. No, all along England has had strong rulers who were determined to show Rome (not Germany, it turns out) who was boss. Including William's descendants, William Rufus and Henry I.

Someone pointed out that even today the Queen appoints bishops, not the other way round, and then someone said that the prime minister even appoints a bishop or two. Double whoa! Can you im-agine, George Bush telling the Baptists what to do? Okay, maybe you can. But seriously, the whole idea of separation of church and state is uniquely American, and we should proudly defend it.

From the Holy Roman Emperor.

May 15, 2006

A Martyr to Excessive Sensibility

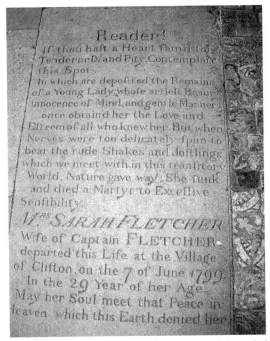

The inspiration for Jane Austen's Sense and Sensibility?

ON MY CLASS FIELD TRIP to Dorchester the other day, I came across this inscription, on a grave inside Dorchester Abbey:

Reader! If thou hast a Heart fam'd for Tenderness and Pity, Contemplate this Spot:

In which are deposited the Remains of a Young Lady whose artless Beauty, innocence of Mind, and gentle Manners once obtain'd her the

Love and Esteem of all who knew her. But when Nerves were too delicately spun to bear the rude Shakes and Jostlings which we meet with in this transitory World, Nature gave way. She sunk and died a Martyr to Excessive Sensibility.

Mrs SARAH FLETCHER Wife of Captain FLETCHER departed this Life at the Village of Clifton on the 7 of June 1799 in the 29 year of her Age May her Soul meet that Peace in Heaven which this Earth denied her.

Sounds like someone needed diazepam.

If you examine the photo you will see that many of the f's are meant to be s's, with "sunk" spelled "funk." I'm not sure why this is— some sort of lexigraphical correction for the lisp?

Also, the tiles to the right are from the late Norman period. They're still vibrant, almost a thousand years later.

January 19, 2007

Warning: Being Stupid Leads to Laryngitis

I STARTED A NEW CLASS at Oxford today, this time on Arthurian Literature. (Remember to pronounce this "litrachure," as is proper when at Oxford.)

I think I'm the only one in the class with no medieval literature cred. It's going to be even harder than usual not to come off as an idiot whenever I open my mouth, so I've decided to pretend I have a sore throat for the duration. "Can't talk, sorry," I'll croak whenever anyone looks my way, trying all the while to appear as if I have loads to say on the contradictions that underscore *Le Morte D'Arthur.*

One guy in the class actually went on about the "corpus of Arthurian literature" when he introduced himself. Another compared King Arthur to Churchill. A woman rather adoringly compared him to Christ. I compared him to Harry Potter.

See what I mean? (Fortunately, no one in the class was present in my last class when I wondered aloud why the Holy Roman Emperor was allowed to marry.)

Must practice: "Sorry, can't talk. Laryngitis."

July 20, 2007

Segueing into Stonor

Stonor, scene of political and religious intrigue, I like to think.

ON WEDNESDAY, a friend invited me to visit Stonor, a manor house near Henley-on-Thames. The house, unlike many old stately homes, has remained in the same family for 850 years. Quite a feat, especially considering the family is Catholic.

The martyr St Edmond Campion hid out here in the 16th century, and here he secretly printed "Ten Reasons" for why Catholicism should be preferred to the new English church. That, as you can imagine, didn't go over very well, but still the Stonor family was able to hang on to their property.

These days, when even the prime minister flirts with Catholicism, Stonor bears no stigma, and during our visit not even, literally, a full-blown cloud. During two months a year, visitors can twice weekly tour the house and grounds, which include an extensive park, a garden, a chapel, a prehistoric stone circle and the most gorgeous copper beech tree I've ever seen. In the summer, Stonor hosts the Summer Proms concerts on the front lawn.

This visit fit nicely with a book I just finished, *An Instance of the Fingerpost* by Iain Pears, a fascinating tale of mystery, history, and science set in 1663 Oxford. It's been compared with Eco's *The Name of the Rose*, but I found it much more readable than Rose. Told by four rather unreliable narrators, it sheds light ever so slowly on a murder and subsequent execution, as well as the political intrigue that surrounded Charles II's restoration to the throne. Peopled by famous scientists and thinkers of the day including Robert Boyle, John Locke, the mathematician John Wallis, Christopher Wren, and John Aubrey, *An Instance of the Fingerpost* reads like a particularly entertaining history text. But it's also a cracking good mystery.

Walking around Stonor, which must have been the scene of more than one heated religious debate, I couldn't help but imagine John Wallis peering around corners, searching for stray Papists.

Now, how was that for a segue?

July 31, 2007

1066

In 1066, this hillside hosted a world-changing battle.

ON SUNDAY WE MADE A pilgrimage to Battle, where the invasion of 1066 took place, near Hastings. Ever since I took a class on the Normans I've been wanting to go, so I dragged the family out with me.

I don't know if you've ever wondered what today's world would have been like if William the Conqueror hadn't been successful in his bid to usurp the throne of England from Harold, but I think about that all the time. (Which perhaps indicates that I have too much time on my hands, although I like to think it's just a vivid imagination.)

Harold Godwinson was a pretty good king, one who'd acted almost as regent under the pious Edward the Confessor. William, the Duke of Normandy and descendant of Vikings, was a bastard in all the ways that counted. Having been promised the throne by Edward years before, he was furious when Harold, Edward's nephew, took it instead. It didn't take him long (or too much gold) to raise an army and receive the pope's blessing.

While William waited in France for the prevailing winds to blow him across the channel, England was invaded from the north by Harold Hardrada of Norway, aligned with Harold's brother Tostig. (All those Harolds probably sent the poor scribes mad.) Harold rushed to defeat them at Stamford Bridge, but had hardly rested from his victory when he heard that William had landed at Pevensey.

His troops worn out, Harold nevertheless rushed back south to face William and defend the crown. But his tired men were defeated after a whole day of fighting on a steep hillside that's now one of the most famous battlefields in the world.

If you go, there's an exhibition centre with a film narrated by David Starkey. The audio guide is also a good listen, properly casting doubt on the notion that Harold was shot in the eye by an arrow.

After William defeated Harold at Hastings, he slowly circled southern England, subduing the local populace as he went. Finally the leaders of London met him at Berkhamsted and offered him the crown of England. Even then he still spent numerous campaigns subduing the northern counties. Vast parts of Yorkshire and Northumberland were listed as "waste" in the Domesday Book of 1086, due to the "harrying" of the North that William was responsible for. (Proving that British understatement was practiced even before the British Isles were united.)

So what would have happened if Harold and his men had been a little more rested?

If William hadn't been victorious that day, the Anglo-Saxons would have continued to rule England. The legal system that the Normans instituted, the basis of English common law, wouldn't exist, nor would the feudal system the Normans were so fond of have flourished. Women, who had more rights under the Anglo-Saxons, probably wouldn't have had to wait another 850 years before finally gaining the right to vote. The Anglo-Saxons were also great artists and artisans, responsible for the beautifully illustrated religious texts now in the British Library.

Had the Normans not stamped out everything Anglo-Saxon, imposing their own Norman French customs and language on England, our language too would be quite different. Modern English is full of Norman-influenced words, giving us more synonyms than most writers know what to do with: female instead of the Anglo-Saxon woman, cottage instead of hut, profound instead of deep, ponderous instead of weighty. Our language is incredibly nuanced because of its Norman influence.

For this, we can thank William, but I don't imagine the Anglo-Saxons who felt his sword that day, or during the years of Norman rule afterward, would be grateful for a few extra synonyms.

October 4, 2007

Old Stuff

TODAY WAS THE FIRST DAY of classes, for me anyway. I'm starting a new course at Oxford, The Architecture of London and the Home Counties.

What are the Home Counties, you ask? Berkshire, Buckinghamshire, Hertfordshire, and Surrey.

But why are they called that, you wonder. I've no idea. Maybe it sounds better than Bedroom Counties.

Anyway, we started out on an auspicious note. When the instructor asked what was the oldest thing in London, several people guessed the Temple of Mithras, the city wall, etc. But I knew immediately it was Cleopatra's Needle. Score one for the home team.

I am still attempting to make up for the London Bridge debacle. (There is, apparently, a vicious rumour around here that the Arizonans thought they were buying the more picturesque Tower Bridge.)

March 10, 2008

The Sir John Soane Museum

WHEN I HAD A PAPER TO WRITE for my literature class, I went to Tintagel, in Cornwall, for inspiration. (At least, that was a good excuse.) So with a paper due on London architecture, I went to the Sir John Soane Museum in Lincoln's Inn Field, just south of Holborn tube stop.

Sir John Soane was a 18th/19th century architect and collector (not the Sir Sloane who contributed his collection to the British Museum; that was someone else). He spent many years in Italy, collecting objects of antiquity and learning the basics of Classical design. The Bank of England is perhaps his greatest achievement, at least of his plans that came to fruition. He built a model for the Houses of Parliament that never was built—you can see it, as well as the drawings, in his museum, and it looks nothing at all like the Gothic building that houses Parliament now.

But there's another common structure in London that is recognized by everyone, and owes its shape, at least, to Soane, despite the fact it wasn't created until many years after he died. The red telephone booth, with its Classical shape, was inspired by the vault that Soane built for his burial at St Pancras Old Church.

Also in the museum, which was once the home of Soane and his wife, is the Picture Room, where a series of paintings by William Hogarth hang: A Rake's Progress and An Election. If you're lucky, while you're in the Picture Room a docent will open the walls, to show yet another layer of paintings, and then yet again, to allow you to peek over into the Monk's Parlour and Yard. There you'll find the grave of Fanny, Mrs. Soane's little dog, whose pictures hang in the Breakfast Room.

The place is stuffed full of Soane's extensive collection (don't miss the Canalettos), and special exhibitions showcase some of his drawings and paintings not on display in the main part of the museum. It reminded me of a Wisconsin tourist attraction called House on the Rock, which was also built by an architect with too large a collection. Except the Soane Museum is not quite as, err, cheesy.

If you go to the Soane Museum, go on a sunny day: the only lighting is from the domed skylights, which floods the basement level through the floor grates. The museum, which is spread across three houses where Soane lived and taught and entertained prospective clients, is small, and entrance is limited. You may have to queue to get in. We arrived around 11 and had a ten minute wait.

Entrance is free, but donations are encouraged. Photographs are not allowed inside, nor are large bags. It's well worth a visit—don't hang around waiting for an excuse.

March 14, 2008

Remember the Bombs

THIS IS ST CLEMENT DANES CHURCH, located on The Strand, just west of the Royal Courts of Justice. It was heavily damaged in the war (when people say "the war" here, they mean World War II) and one wall was intentionally left with its damage intact.

Yesterday in class we saw a map of London with the bomb damaged areas in black, purple and orange. Vast swaths of London were black and purple. St Paul's was surrounded by purple bomb damage but miraculously escaped all but a minor (orange) hit to the portico. (The populace were not informed of this, in an effort to maintain morale.) One woman in class remembered her home in Wandsworth being destroyed; fortunately she was staying with her grandmother a few blocks away when it happened.

I've heard many similar stories from people here, all of whom obviously survived. Looking at yesterday's map reminded me again of how many didn't, and how much of London was destroyed by the very unsmart bombs of the Germans.

For me, having grown up in the US where bombs never drop out of the skies at night, it's hard to understand how people could have lived like this, sleeping under staircases for fear the house would collapse around them. A whole generation here, however, remembers that very vividly.

St Clement Danes is a reminder, for the rest of us.

St Clement Danes' pock marked exterior, a reminder of the damage of war.

July 27, 2008

Althorp: Another Piece of History

Currently celebrating 500 years of history, Althorp is a reminder that history is made every day.

ON SATURDAY I VISITED ANOTHER "stately home" as they're known here—this one rather more stately than most, as it's the seat of Earl Spencer. As always, visiting these places isn't just an opportunity to ohh and ahh over the fancy furnishings. It's a visit through history, and for me, another thread in the rich tapestry I'm slowly piecing together during my time here. Everywhere I go, more pieces come together—a portrait, or a painting, reminds me of something I've seen before.

Althorp is a close cousin to Blenheim Palace, where the Churchills live—yes, that Churchill: John Churchill was the first Duke of Marlborough, a great-great-great etc grandfather to Sir Winston Churchill, and an ancestor of the Spencers of Althorp.

While the Churchills are probably the most famous family in England (going back further than the upstart Windsors), the Spencers aren't far behind. One of the Spencers is memorialized at Althorp—you might remember her funeral, watched by millions all over the world.

The Diana Memorial is a peaceful place. Ironically, for a woman who was pursued by the press her whole adult life, her final resting place is an island of solitude—literally. A quiet path meanders down to the pond, which is shared by ducks and geese, but no paparazzi.

There's an exhibit celebrating Diana's life at Althorp, including artifacts from her childhood and some of her dresses, as well as the specially fitted outfit she wore as she inspected landmine fields as part of her humanitarian work.

Althorp is located about an hour north of London, near Northampton. As I passed by the entrance gates, I remembered when I'd seen them before: after the funeral of Diana eleven years ago, when the hearse was filmed on its route from Westminster Abbey, being bombarded with bouquets tossed by mourners and followed, one last time, by the media.

Just another day in history.

August 22, 2009

Time Traveling to Jane Austen's House

Jane Austen's house in Chawton, Hampshire

IT'S TERRIFICALLY EASY, I've discovered, to time travel in England. All you need is a bit of imagination and a working knowledge of Britain's rail and road system. Last week I journeyed to the late Victorian period at the Linley Sambourne house in Kensington, and on Thursday I traveled to the Regency period during a visit to Jane Austen's house in Chawton, Hampshire.

First, a bit on the major eras in British history, useful info for time traveling novices: In Britain, periods are generally named after the monarch who reigned during the time. The Victorian Period, used to describe furniture styles as well as history, was between 1837, when Victoria came to the throne, and 1901, when she died. The Regency Period spans the years 1811 and 1820, and is named after the regency of George IV, who ruled when his father, George III, became unfit. The period before that is named after three successive Georges, the Georgian Period.

The Regency period is particularly fascinating to historical novelists. An entire genre in American literature, the Regency Romance, characterized by Georgette Heyer, is named for the brief but exciting period. Not only was there a war going on with Napoleon, which presents writers with the possibility of plenty of tortured war heroes, but Romantic poets like Byron and Shelley were obligingly penning love poetry. London and cities like Bath began to look more like a romanticized ancient Greece, thanks to architects like John Nash and Robert Adam. Unlike the later Victorian period, morals were looser and pleasure seeking was considered a perfectly acceptable pastime. London Society was occupied with balls, parties, and gambling, while in Brighton the Prince Regent was building his over-the-top Pavilion.

And in an idyllic setting in Hampshire, Jane Austen was writing sparkling dialogue and cutting commentary that continues to inspire authors and screenwriters today.

Jane Austen's family were poor. But by a fortunate twist of fate that seems torn from the pages of a novel, her brother Edward was adopted by rich distant relations. When he inherited the estates, he allowed his mother and sisters to live at the house in Chawton, which today is open to the public and furnished with many original Austen pieces.

Jane sat at this tiny table and wrote her novels.

It's not a fabulous mansion, like the one where Edward lived up the road. Nor is it extravagantly furnished—in fact, the writing table where Jane penned her novels is very small, hardly the sort of desk from which you'd imagine great Literature bursting forth. But it is comfortable and spacious. It's easy to picture Jane, her sister Cassandra, and their mother filling their hours here, making tea on the hob, climbing the stairs to their bedrooms, or gazing out the window as their neighbors' donkey carts passed by.

The original square Clementi piano is still in the drawing room, along with a bureau belonging to Mr. Austen. In the room Jane shared with her sister is a replica of her bed, as well as a lace shawl belonging to her niece, Fanny. Did Jane lie in a bed like this, dreaming of Elinor and Marianne Dashwood's heartbreak and happiness?

The gardens have been carefully recreated and feature plants that would have been found in a Regency garden—no exotic Victorian specimens from Asia. A dye garden, with plants used for dyes, is blooming like mad in August. Would Jane have sat in the shade of the large oak tree and imagined the Bennet girls falling in love?

Chawton House Library

A short walk up the road is the Chawton House Library. The house where Jane's wealthy brother, Edward Knight (he changed his name after being adopted), lived is now owned by an American, who's opened it as a home to early English women's literature. Guided tours of the house are available on Tuesday and Thursday. On the grounds of the estate is the churchyard where Jane's sister and mother are buried—both lived to be very old.

Jane Austen's house is open most of the year (weekends only in January and February). Photos (without flash) are allowed inside the house, a rarity in Britain.

If you're traveling by car rather than time traveling, you'll find Chawton 13 miles south of Basingstoke, near Alton on the A339. And you'll find Jane Austen's books at your library or bookstore.

January 25, 2010

The Limes of Ancient Rome

I STARTED A NEW CLASS last week, Latter Days of Roman Britain. The instructor helpfully handed out a sheet with names, places, and other unfamiliar terms listed in two columns. As he lectured, I noticed he was going in order: Ceasar, Atrebates, Icini, Boudica, etc. With about twenty words in each column, I figured he'd finish the list just as class was over.

The very last word was "limes." I was excited to hear about the Romans' use of limes. Did they eat them to prevent scurvy? Did they suck them with their ale? Did they prefer the taste of lime to lemon?

I waited impatiently as the final words on the list went by: Stracathro, Dacia, Decebalus, Parthia. (The Romans were having trouble in Germany.) It was time to leave, but the instructor kept going, thankfully—I didn't want to miss the limes part.

Finally, fifteen minutes after class was officially over, he got to "limes." Turns out it wasn't a tangy fruit at all. It was "lim-es," the Latin word for "wall." The Romans were fond of building walls around their territory.

Once again, I left class feeling foolish, I daresay even green.

March 29, 2009

A Timely Visit to Blenheim Palace

The Clock Tower at Blenheim Palace, one of many outdoor clocks.

THERE ARE LOTS OF CLOCKS at Blenheim Palace. Some are on the outside of the palace; many more are on the inside. What struck me during my visit today was that all of them were correct—an amazing feat, since last night, all clocks went forward an hour as Europe switched to Daylight Savings Time (British Summer Time here). I guess when you're the Duke of Marlborough you have no problem finding someone to change all the clocks in your home, even if your home, covering seven acres, is larger than most villages.

Unlike other palaces, Blenheim Palace is not a royal residence. It was built by a grateful nation to honor John Churchill for his victory in the War of Spanish Secession, which saved Europe from the clutches of the evil Sun King, Louis XIV. Only problem was, Queen

Anne got pissed off at Churchill's wife, Sarah, who'd been her favorite, halfway through the building and cut off funding for the construction of Blenheim. Fortunately it was too late to take back the dukedom she'd granted Churchill, the First Duke of Marlborough.

Interestingly, his oldest daughter Henrietta inherited the dukedom after his death, as his two sons had previously died. She became Duchess, and after her death, the dukedom went to her nephew Charles, the grandson of John Churchill. He was the ancestor of Winston Churchill while his brother John was the ancestor of Princess Diana and her brother, Earl Spencer.

Got that?

The interior of the palace is pretty fabulous, in an early-18th century way. Much of the furnishings were paid for, however, by an American, the 9th Duchess, Consuela Vanderbilt, whose fortune bought back much of the wealth that had been sold in the 19th century.

If the palace looks vaguely familiar, perhaps you've seen it in the film *The Young Victoria*. Its front forecourt doubled as Buckingham Palace while the library played the part of Prince Albert's uncle's palace in Belgium. This was indeed a timely visit, as the exhibit on the film, currently on display in the library, ends on March 31.

Blenheim Palace, a UNESCO World Heritage Site, is located about 20 minutes northwest of Oxford, on the A44 (about an hour and a half from London). You can tour the palace, or simply walk the grounds, which allow dogs on leads. The grounds and gardens were designed by Capability Brown, one of England's great landscape artists.

July 4, 2013

Happy Independence Day! All Is Forgotten.

A bust of King George at Kew Palace

The history of the present King of Great Britain is a history of repeated injuries and usurpations, all having in direct object the establishment of an absolute Tyranny over these States. —Thomas Jefferson, The Declaration of Independence, 1776

IT'S INDEPENDENCE DAY in the United States, the day that the colonies declared their independence from their British overlords. Or was that actually the 2nd of July?

Regardless, the day is greeted with fireworks and fired-up grills in what is now the United States of America. Here in Britain, it's greeted with nothing more than a reminder that stock markets are closed in the US.

I get the sense there's not much lingering animosity over that whole Revolutionary War thing. Maybe because people here are too busy enjoying the benefits of American tourism, especially now that the dollar is high against the pound. Welcome, sneaker wearing American tourists! May your backpacks overflow with Mind the Gap memorabilia!

Or more likely, it will be Royal memorabilia that fills those backpacks. Every American I know (well, every one who comes here) is obsessed with British Royalty. Yes, the descendants of hated George III, who our forefathers rebelled against, are objects of awe to the royalty-deprived Americans.

Sometimes I think if the Founding Fathers knew how Americans would one day go gaga over British Royalty, they wouldn't have bothered. I mean, what do we care about trial by jury and "transporting us beyond Seas" when our self-made celebrities aren't nearly so fascinating?

American media websites are saturated with stories about the eminent Royal birth. There's far more breathless speculation there, in fact, than on British media sites. What is it with Americans' fascination with all things Royal? How soon they forget that whole taxation without representation thing. Those "injuries and usurpations" are just water under the bridge now.

So what if the King plunders our seas, ravages our coasts, burns our towns, and destroys the lives of our people—Kate Middleton's having a baby! And Prince Harry dances so well! And Queen Elizabeth has such a warm, friendly smile, doesn't she? She couldn't possibly want to "transport large Armies of foreign Mercenaries to compleat the works of death, desolation and tyranny." That would be totally unworthy of the Head of a civilized nation.

Ah well. Bygones, and all that. All is forgiven. Because Kate Middleton wears really cool footwear.

I'm actually more fascinated by the dead royals than the living ones. (I even went to see Diana's grave.) I love going to palaces and stately homes, but I care nothing at all about how Kate is decorating her Kensington Palace digs.

As long as she and Wills don't plan to "Quarter large bodies of armed troops among us," I'm cool.

Despite the fact our blood runs red, white and blue, we don't do much celebrating here. Our Irish dog doesn't appreciate the fireworks, although he might appreciate the sentiment of Independence Day. We'll probably take him for a walk, let him run free in honor of the day we tore off the choke collar of our English tyrants.

Now, don't go "cutting off our trade with all parts of the world" while our backs are turned.

CHAPTER FIVE

A Plucky Seafaring Nation

Britain is an island nation, surrounded by seas, channels and oceans. Plus, there's a lot of rain. Dealing with water, whether pouring from the skies or in the form of high seas is second nature to Brits. Some manage better than others.

February 8, 2005

You Row, Girl!

THE ISLES ARE ALL ATWITTER today as Ellen MacArthur is expected to pull into Falmouth any hour now, after setting the round-the-world solo-sailing record last night somewhere off the coast of France—71 days, 14 hours, 18 minutes and 33 seconds after starting her journey. She returns a hero, though tempered by criticisms of her constant "whinging" (whining?) on her blog. (Hey, it's hard enough blogging every single day, without having to contend with doldrums, 30 foot waves, and obstructionist fish!)

There were also complaints that her journey, sponsored by B&Q hardware stores, was so high tech it hardly counted as human achievement, that her journal entries describing an encounter with a whale weren't quite up to Melville. And worse, that her lack of a stiff upper lip, illustrated by her online "psycho babble," might have permanently damaged the national psyche.

Whatever.

For those who can't get behind Ellen, here's another hero, another British woman who braved the wide sea on her own, but in a rowboat, not a high tech "trimaran" with GPS positioning, a Royal Air Force helo hovering overhead, and 12 webcams.

Debra Veal set off in 2001 to row across the Atlantic in the Ward Evans Atlantic Rowing Challenge, accompanied by her husband Andrew, an experienced rower. Though she'd only learned to row in the last year, she looked forward to the challenge, and a little time alone with hubby.

Nine days later, her husband left the boat after coming down with an uncontrollable fear of the ocean. She continued alone, battling the sea, dodging supertankers, and befriending sea turtles. Here's an excerpt from her Top Ten Worst Moments:

Troika Transatlantic Diary Continued:

5. Day 19 - Had a shark under the boat that night, chasing fish. As I watched the trail of glowing phosphorescence as it swam at high speeds I convinced myself that it was going to attack the boat so I hid in the cabin, very scared until dawn.

4. Day 14 - The day Andrew left the boat. As I watched the yacht sail towards us on its way to pick up Andrew we held each other and cried. I couldn't help thinking that if anything went wrong we might never see each other again.

3. Ten days of unbearable loneliness at the start of December, which climaxed on day 65 when I cried from 8am till 11am, until I finally plucked up enough strength to get out of the cabin and row. My diary that day reads, "wind was so strong, fighting the waves kept on making me dissolve into tears. I'm so exhausted and just want to sleep".

2. Day 23 - Everything seemed to be going wrong then I nearly got run down by a super tanker. I wrote in my diary, "I am at an all time low and don't know if I am going to be able to recover... I'm so scared and I want to go home".

Debra lost the race; in fact, not only did she come in last—111 days after starting, 69 days behind the winning team—but she was also disqualified.

Whatever.

She's got my vote for "Pluckiest Seafaring Brit Since Francis Drake" and my admiration, and who cares if she doesn't describe her encounter with a sea turtle quite the way Melville would?

Read her diary and laugh, cry, and whinge with her:

6. *Day 54 - First day of surfing really big waves. I wrote in my diary, "It was awesome - I LOVE IT!". That evening my face ached from grinning so much.*

Now there's a stiff upper lip!

July 24, 2006

Four Girls in a Boat*

River voyages are not to be undertaken lightly.

WE WENT TO OXFORD YESTERDAY, a journey that was not without its perils. Roadworks on the A40 have resulted in massive traffic tie-ups that seem to get longer every time I travel to Oxford. I suspect the same cars are just piling up, mile upon mile, day after day. It took an hour to get through the roadworks, whereas last time it took only 20 minutes. (That's right, I said "only." Traffic jams here usually include bottles of water airdropped by helicopter on hot days, free coffees during the winter months.) But I had convinced the girls we should try our hand at punting. So once we got there, we headed for Magdalen Bridge (pronounced "maudlin") where we managed to procure a punt. (£12 an hour, plus deposit and proof of sanity.)

A punt is a flat-bottomed boat about the size of a canoe, but instead of rowing with paddles you pole it around from behind. (Rivers in England aren't very deep; this would never work in the Atchafalaya River, for instance.) They also provided a paddle, for steering, or maybe just to avoid the proverbial analogies to a certain creek.

As we boarded the boat, I ordered Daughter Number One's friend, who looked like a strong girl, to swallow her ice cream cone and grab the pole. But the rest of the crew quickly lost confidence in her leadership and mutinied. DNO took over, and she proved an excellent, if somewhat bossy, skipper. It did take her a while to get the steering thing figured out: we floated around in gentle circles while our fellow punters laughed at us, offering friendly tips. I reverted to dog training mode: "Good girl!" I shouted whenever she managed to get us headed in the right direction. "Shut up!" she barked back, "and paddle in the OTHER direction!" (You've heard of seasickness? I have sea dyslexia. Remember this term if they institute the draft.)

By the time we'd gone halfway round the route they'd outlined for us on the map she seemed to be in fine form, although I could tell from observing the other punters that she was facing the wrong way, employing more of a shoving action than a propelling one. But we brazened it out. "We're Americans," we shouted to the other punters, in case they didn't guess from our accents. "We own the seas!" (Okay, we didn't say that. Probably because most of the other punters were Americans too. We own the airlines.)

The voyage did not prove to be without obstacle: forget those images of gently floating along the river, a plastic cup of champagne in your hand, the quiet sounds of water sloshing against the bow (or is that a prow?) while a nocturne plays in the background. (We really did hear a nocturne, at one point, coming from one of the nearby buildings. This is Oxford, remember.) It was a little more like shooting the rapids in the Rockies, except instead of dangerous shoals we had dangerous foliage, which for some reason they have allowed to line the banks of the Cherwell. Like a siren, it lures novice punters to its green depths, entangling them in thorny limbs...you get the picture.

Foliage on the banks of the River Cherwell impedes our progress.

Daughter Number Two was along, too, but she was more or less an impressed sailor. She doesn't like water, she informed me as soon as she'd taken her seat in the punt. In fact she hates it, she told me a minute later. Further, she didn't want to be there, she added as we lodged ourselves firmly against one of the docked punts. When we nudged against the sloping riverbank I offered to look the other way while she went AWOL but she refused to abandon the ship. (I think it was the education benefits we'd promised her.)

When we finally made land, we were all a bit grumpy with each other. This may be an indication that long sea voyages are not a good idea, at least not for landlubbers like us. I'm much more at home with a steering wheel and anti-lock brakes. We were, however, pretty proud that we'd returned mostly undamaged, except for the scratches from the foliage and wet bottoms. As we floated gently under Magdalen Bridge, careful to avoid ramming it this time, another punter almost hit us. "Sorry about that," he shouted. "It's our first time!"

"It was ours too, an hour ago," I told him, with an encouraging smile. "You'll get the hang of it!" Then, as he propelled his punt toward the center of the Cherwell, I called out, "Good boy!"

*Not to be confused with the book *Three Men in a Boat* by Jerome K. Jerome, which if you haven't read you simply must. Especially if you have any intention of taking to the high seas.

February 25, 2006

Welcome to Sealand, Population 5 Geeks

LAST WEEKEND I WROTE about Andorra, a tiny nation located in the mountains between France and Spain. I said then that Andorra wasn't the smallest country in the world; in fact, compared to Sealand, a tiny micronation off the coast of Britain, it's a veritable superpower.

Sealand is about the size of a football pitch and has a permanent population of around five. Like Andorra, Sealand is a tax haven but unlike sheep-dotted Andorra, it's also a dot.com center of high tech (if shady) internet commerce. (But if you think your spam is coming from Sealand, think again; they maintain strict controls on the types of internet activity allowed to emanate from Sealand. No kiddie porn, and no spam.) Not only are there no sheep in Sealand; there's no grass there either. (I don't mean THAT kind of grass.) It's basically a rusty steel deck suspended over concrete piers, with sleeping facilities and, I'm betting, a latte machine.

Sealand was established when the current Prince Paddy Roy Bates settled on the deserted WWII sea fort Roughs Tower with his family. He survived several coup attempts, including the efforts of the British government to claim sovereignty of the fortress. One of the nastier coups involved the kidnapping of Prince Michael, who was 15 and alone on the island at the time. Prince Roy, with the help of a helicopter stunt pilot, reclaimed the island from the Dutch and German duo who'd captured it, later negotiating their release with their respective governments. (Incidentally, Sealand abides by the rules of the Geneva Convention, unlike other principalities I could name.)

You may have heard of Sealand, or seen one of its fake passports. Do not be fooled: Sealand only issues passports to legitimate friends of the government, and would never sell them over the internet. It has a national anthem, "E Mare Libertas," which is really quite a catchy tune.

The US refuses to recognize Sealand (or maybe no one in the State Department's heard of it yet—they've been too busy invading other assorted nation states) but then they don't recognize Taiwan either. No biggie.

After looking at photos of Sealand (available via Google.com), you may be wondering how one actually arrives on this sea fortress. (Physically, I mean. It's next to impossible to get a visa.) There's a helo-pad, but I've learned it is impossible to land there without permission, due to the defences erected by the principality: namely a large pole in the middle. It's simple, really: you are hoisted up via a large swing, which is likely to be the most excitement you'll have during your stay in Sealand.

Despite the inhospitable environs, Sealand, I must admit, inspires my sense of whimsy, just as Andorra did many years ago. It would be a great setting for a novel, I think. Just imagine a cartoon cover with a Bridget Jones-like character, arriving on Sealand for a fun filled weekend with Prince Michael and some computers. I could see Clive Owen as the lead...

November 20, 2006

Warnings of Gales

THIS MORNING'S SHIPPING FORECAST, which I listen to most mornings at 5:30 despite having no intention of taking to the high seas, is full of dire gale warnings, even a Force 12 here and there. The announcer, as usual, lists the maritime conditions matter-of-factly, but I detect a tone of glee as he predicts a "vigorous depression" heading our way.

This is not the sort of news that will get people out of bed, surprisingly.

Instead I lie there, grateful I'm not in water-locked Bailey, where there's Violent Storm 11 expected, occasionally Hurricane Force 12 in South, decreasing 7 to Severe Gale 9 later. I imagine sailors, battening down their hatches, scurrying to hoist the mainsail, or whatever sailors do during Violent Storm 11s. Pray, probably.

Maybe they'll make for Rockall, where they'll find conditions a little better: Squally showers, moderate or poor. Too bad there are no warm pubs on Rockall, or even permanent human settlements.

I contemplate heading to Faeroes, Cyclonic 7 to Severe Gale 9, but I suspect I'd need a passport and a sturdy windbreaker. Fair Isle, despite the optimistic name, will see occasional outbreaks of Violent Storm 11 as well. Best head south, if you're in charge of the rudder.

Today's a good day to be a Lundian, or whatever residents of Lundy call themselves. They've no gales in the forecast, and have organized themselves with a proper pub or two. Must have somewhere to bring the odd shipwrecked sailor.

The Inshore Waters Forecast delivers better news, though Cape Wrath is in for rough seas. What do they expect, naming the place after an emotional outburst?

The Inshore Waters Forecast is where things get really interesting. I lie there, waiting for the announcer to get tripped up when he comes to Ardnamurchan Point. But he successfully navigates the diphthongs of the Scottish waters. I'm relieved, and wide awake now after my tempestuous roller-coaster ride around the British Isles.

It's days like this when I'm glad to be a landlubber, with nothing more challenging to my maritime safety than a moderate puddle here and there.

CHAPTER SIX

Neighbourly?

I don't always feel welcome in Britain. Or even very neighbourly. Is it something I said?

July 1, 2005

How Much Does Dirt Weigh?

This sign at the Tesco construction site makes sense now.

YESTERDAY I WAS IN LONDON, meeting with other expat bloggers. I also went to St Paul's Cathedral, which will be significant in a moment.

(No, I didn't have a conversion.)

When I arrived at Marylebone to catch a train home, the marquee was blank. I thought I'd missed the last train but then they announced an even bigger disaster: the train tunnel at my town collapsed. No one was hurt, but there were plenty of out-of-sorts commuters. (We bonded, however, on the replacement bus, though it was a little eerie. I felt like I was heading for some kind of upscale gulag with my fellow passengers, on a coach with photos of Queen

Elizabeth's Golden Jubilee taped to the inside. Sometimes you don't ask questions.)

As for that wayward tunnel, I have my theories. Before I moved here Tesco received permission to build a supermarket in this small town, after much local opposition. It's being built right over the train tracks, which required a tunnel to be built. They finally finished constructing the tunnel, and the other day I noticed they'd filled the dirt in over it.

"That's a lot of dirt," I thought. "I wonder if that tunnel will collapse one day."

(No, I still haven't had a conversion. Just a prescient moment.)

We've had a lot of rain lately, and when dirt gets wet it becomes heavier. I guess the engineers who designed this didn't factor that in, being as Tesco was in a hurry to open the store and start making a profit.

Which brings to mind another theory. The local grocer, A.A. Fisher, will likely go out of business when the new Tesco opens. Nah....

And the St Paul's connection? While I was inside the cathedral, I marveled at the mastery of architecture and engineering Christopher Wren must have had to build such a monument 300 years ago, probably without Mathematica on his laptop, even. He was in his early thirties at the time, yet had been a practicing architect since he was a teenager.

I know some commuters who wish he were around today.

August 29, 2005

Dear Neighbours

DEAR FELLOW RESIDENTS of my formerly Tranquil & Bucolic Underworld,

Your party last night put me in a very bad mood. I don't know if you had an actual live band in your garden, or a DJ with some honking amps and a hearing problem, but your music throbbed in my eardrums while I was trying to sleep since SOME OF US HAVE TO GET UP MONDAY MORNING.

Your house is located several hundred yards from my house, and there are many trees between us, so I shouldn't have had to be bombarded by the sounds of your Gomorrah in full swing. But because you chose to violate the codes of conduct we normally observe here in Residential Land by pumping out decibels reserved for discos—no, not even West End clubs play music that loud OUTDOORS—I had to listen to your stupid thumping bass when I'd rather have been sleeping (as I normally do between eleven and midnight). Not even my thick walls, which keep this house cool on the hottest summer days, could keep out the sound of your horrid music—by the way, have you any idea what decade this is?

I don't give a rat's ass what you were celebrating. A wedding, most likely. Such occasions happen every day in an orderly manner and there is no need to throw a huge party that clogs up residential lanes with big ass cars and violates noise ordinances. Your inconsiderate behaviour will no doubt bring bad karma to the newlyweds. If not, the curse I've placed on you and your house will cause your testicles to shrivel and your plumbing to back up. (With raw sewage, should these things go as planned, which they hardly ever do—but still, it should be enough to ensure a few sleepless hours for you and yours.)

Let this serve as a notice to the rest of my neighbours: Should you violate the quiet of this neighbourhood with anything other than Guy Fawkes fireworks or the occasional whoop of joy at having passed your A Levels, the Third Ring of Hell shall be as nothing compared to my wrath.

Signed, Sleepless and Grumpy, and her faithful dog Cerberus

P.S. Bah. Humbug.

(Disclaimer: This author does not condone, etc., violence, etc. or even, in fact, believe in curses.)

March 23, 2006

Stranger in a Strange Land

I WAS TALKING to a sweet-looking little old lady at the Common this morning, and naturally we were discussing whether or not it would rain, which led to comments about the water shortage we've been warned about, which led to her telling me our water shortage problems were due to the fact that there were just too many people here.

There are, she said, too many foreigners living here.

A few minutes later she asked, "Are you from America?" and I said yes, but there was no mention of whether I was one of the foreigners she was talking about.

Nevertheless, I shall try not to use too much water.

May 30, 2006

In Which I Journey to Wales and Barely Avoid Fisticuffs

YESTERDAY WE WENT TO the Hay Festival in Hay-on-Wye, to see Al Gore give his talk about climate change. Book festivals here aren't like the ones in the States, where authors are so eager for exposure they talk for free. At Hay, you have to pay for each author event you attend. But apparently that doesn't keep out the ill-mannered riff-raff like the man sitting behind me.

He was British, and I overheard him say that he liked Al Gore because he was "so articulate, for an American." This was because, he told his wife (who I never heard say a word—I guess she wasn't very articulate), that Al Gore traveled a lot, whereas most senators didn't even have passports. (Now, I know one senator has bragged about not having a passport, but the others must surely be using passports when they travel to their overseas boondoggles.)

It's true that Americans don't travel as much as their British cousins. Brits are constantly catching EasyJet flights to the Canary Islands, Spain, Mallorca, or else Majorca, Spain, and generally anywhere with sun and a beach, like Spain (where you can get a full English breakfast just about anywhere). My neighbors have a house in Spain, where they spend their summers, but as far as I can tell it hasn't improved either their English or their Spanish. They are, however, articulate, almost as much so as the man sitting behind me.

I guess all that sun does wonders for the articulation.

What I wanted to tell this man was that most Americans, a) can't afford to travel abroad. A ticket to Europe costs far more than EasyJet fare to Barcelona. Most Americans don't have the disposable incomes that the average European does, and what little they do have goes to save for a medical emergency, not for inflated London hotel prices.

And b) most Americans don't take days off for something like travel. We don't have bank holidays, or even in most cases more than two weeks vacation (and many Americans spend even that at work). British children—and often their parents—get long breaks every season: the last spring break was 19 days. I know of very few American professionals (who are the only ones who can afford overseas flights) who would want to spend 19 days away from their jobs, even if their Scrooge bosses offered it to them. Our ancestors, remember, were Puritans who left England and subsequently invented the work ethic.

And further, if we do wish to travel, there are lots of places in the Americas where we can travel without a passport. Six Flags, despite coming under the province of six nations, doesn't require a passport, and until recently, neither did Juarez or Montreal. So there are lots of well-traveled, well-read Americans who—horrors!—don't have a passport.

I took careful note of this man's further discourse, none of which was particularly articulate, despite his tan. Of course, the glare I gave him after his statement might have been enough to stifle any inclinations toward articulation he may have possessed. (I barely refrained from smacking him across the brow. My husband hates it when I break into fisticuffs with the locals.)

I would say something about how all British people are bigots, but I refuse to judge a whole nation of people based on a sample of one. I'm particular like that.

I would go on, but I'm not feeling very articulate right now. Maybe I should go lie in the sun a bit.

August 14, 2006

Meet the Neighbors: Terrorists, Racists, and Stockbrokers

(Written after the liquid bomb scare in August, 2006, which occurred on the day my daughter was scheduled to fly to the United States.)

OUR ALERT STATUS has been downgraded from critical to severe. We can now carry one piece of hand luggage on our flights, but no liquids. The British patience has been sorely tested four days into our transport trial, with airport authorities the targets of the whinging. Flights are still not back to normal, although John Lennon Airport in Liverpool and Robin Hood Airport near Nottingham are experiencing no delays, proving peaceniks and poverty campaigners can at least run airports properly.

Over the weekend we learned some of the suspects were white converts to Islam, residents of the "stockbroker belt" in south Buckinghamshire. I'm not so surprised to find out my neighbors are terrorists, but to realize I'm surrounded by stockbrokers is somewhat unsettling. (I've also heard them called "elderly snobs." I guess that's what happens when stockbrokers retire.)

Now they're scouring the woods near High Wycombe for evidence. If there are explosives in the woods I hope they find them, and while they're at it they should pick up the litter too. The resident stockbrokers don't bother to pick up their rubbish, I've noticed.

This morning someone from the estate agent's office was out here, and as she was leaving she said the solution to our current problem was to stop letting people from other countries into Britain. "Not you, of course," she assured me.

Then she reminded me that years ago everyone here was blond-haired and blue-eyed. (That lets me out; I'm definitely not blonde, and my eyes are just about every color but blue.)

Knowing my neighbors are racists is almost as upsetting as learning they're stockbrokers.

August 21, 2008

Safe As Houses?

Typical Edwardian house, spared demolition—for now.

HAVE YOU HEARD? Britain has a housing crisis. Too many people, too few houses. And nowhere to build a new house. (Except a flood plain. But that's another crisis.)

With the housing market the way it is now in Britain, people don't want to sell, or buy—housing prices have fallen, and may fall further, but they're still extremely high.

So the thing to do, in my neighborhood at least, is to completely gut your house and rebuild. In a half square-mile area, there are at my count six houses undergoing extensive renovation, in one case rebuilding from the ground up. Two are located next door to each other, and another is across the street from those two. A massive renovation project involves several vans, lorries, and other vehicles, all of which must park on a street built for residential traffic only.

The last three times I tried to drive down my street, I had to turn around and detour due to the road being blocked.

It's very annoying, and with the house next door having just sold, I worry that it too could go under the scaffolding and become another reno nightmare.

Many of the houses here were built around the turn of the century—the rail line came out here in 1906, prompting a building boom. Now those houses are worth a small fortune, but not because they're lovely old homes—they are, but they're also sitting on land that's priceless. Zoning laws prohibit new building—unless it's Tesco. So people tear down perfectly good homes and build modern versions of the same house.

The newer houses all fit in the architectural scheme around here—Georgian brick and fake half-timbered houses seem to be the most popular replacement styles.

But they just don't have the well-loved look of the older homes. Inside, they'll have modern kitchens, up-to-date plumbing, and state-of-the-art insulation. It will take far longer for the ivy to climb over the new brick, for the clematis to snake over the siding, than it took to demolish century-old timber.

Britain is a place that adores its past, but sadly, the past is falling victim to posh.

CHAPTER SEVEN

Dog Talk

If I thought moving to England was great, my dog, a Golden Retriever who'd never seen a body of water larger than a bathtub, thought it was fantastic. Off-lead walks through the countryside, along the Thames, and over ancient monuments were all part of the wonderful life available to a dog in England.

January 28, 2005

If You Could Talk to the Animals

I DON'T KNOW WHAT kind of relationship you have with your dog, but mine is caring, rewarding, and built on two-way communication. We have frequent conversations (and before you ask, no, I'm not mentally ill, nor is "dog" a cute reference to my husband). My dog is a three-year-old Golden Retriever and she talks. Not the way we do, but with her eyes, her tail, and a low-throated whine.

Yesterday she was in a talkative mood. First, she told me she wanted a snack. I gave her one, and a few minutes later she mentioned she wanted another. Since her snacks are located in the kitchen, very near my own, I gave her another, and got myself a cookie too.

Then, bolstered by success, she announced she wanted a walk, by whining and looking longingly at the front door.

Wanting to get back to blogging, I tried to distract her. "We'll walk later," I said. "I don't have my shoes on." She looked at the floor, right at my muddy New Balance. "But I don't have your leash—" She turned her head pointedly toward the closet, where the leash hung on the doorknob. No excuse was good enough, and since the sun was clearly shining, I knew I couldn't pull the "It's raining" one over on her either.

We went to the woods, and for once she stuck close to me, since the day before she had been brutally raped in these same woods. The perpetrator was a young Weimaraner, whose operation had apparently left just enough juice for certain animal urges to be acted upon.

This time, only a squirrel teased her, shamelessly waving his tail from the lower branches of a beech tree. Little did he know my dog can climb trees, too, but with memories of the rape still fresh, she was in no mood to display her awesome tree-climbing ability.

When we arrived home, she still wasn't content. I was sitting at my computer, happily blogging away, when she came to the doorway. I ignored her, as I'm trying not to spoil her with attention, but then I heard a thunk.

She'd dropped her brush, not on the carpet, where it wouldn't make a noise, but on the hard floor.

So I stopped blogging and brushed her, and gave her a little massage while I was at it. Thirty minutes later, I went to the kitchen, thinking it might be time for a snack. She followed, and whined again. "WHAT do you want NOW?" I snapped, tired of submitting to her whims. She turned and gazed at the basket of dog treats, not in its usual place atop the fridge, but on the counter. Her gaze didn't waver, but I did. I gave her a treat, then another. (Tomorrow I'll get back to not spoiling the dog.)

What I want to know is, when is she going to start her own blog? Imagine the snark: "Suckered Mom into forking over ten cookies. Even ate the peanut she put out for that wanker squirrel! And get a load of Friday Cat Blogging! Wish I could be in the middle of that!"

February 16, 2005

Reporting for Duty

WE DIDN'T GET to watch the Westminster Kennel Club dog show here, which is just as well. My dog is still mad at me because I didn't register her in the AKC, thus dashing her hopes of being a show dog. (She's seen how many treats those dogs get, and she wants some of that action.)

I'd wanted her to go into pet therapy, but she flunked the test, deliberately, I suspect. She just wasn't cut out for social work. When I eventually sneaked her into the nursing home to visit Grandma, she did think it was pretty cool—Grandma spills a lot of food—but then the menacing sight of a guy in a wheelchair gave her the willies. (That's just unnatural, she says, for people to have wheels.)

Since she loves the snow, she decided she wanted to be a rescue dog like her brother (the pick of the litter, he moved to Colorado and trained in Search and Rescue). I took her to agility school, but the preparation was for naught. Turns out there aren't too many opportunities to rescue people from dangerous teeter totters in the actual wild.

After we moved to Britain, the land of pampered pooches, she thought she might like to be a Yorkshire terrier, but they took one look at her and ruled her ineligible. (Something about tail docking—WTF?!) Besides, those cute plaid coats don't come in extra large, and what's the point of being a toy breed if cool threads don't come with the job?

On her first outing in Regent's Park, she was attracted to the water, which offered several exciting career possibilities—a swim instructor? A lifeguard? Diving for tennis balls? But then a swan spit at her and a career on the high seas was out.

Our new house in the country presented an opportunity as a guard dog...until she got her first close-up look at the cows in the neighboring pasture. ("Those things are HUGE! Mommy! That one LOOKED at me! Help!")

Now she's decided undercover work is for her. Every time she goes outside, she rolls in the mud, cleverly disguising herself as a sewer rat. The enemy? Apparently it's the pair of Commie ducks nesting next door. (You didn't know ducks were communist? *Make Way for Ducklings* was set in Boston. What more proof do you need?)

I try to tell her we're vegan, and all the animals are our friends, but she's not buying it. She's read *Animal Farm*, and knows it's just a matter of time until they organize a resistance, and as a Tool of Man she'll be first on their list for extinction.

I hear retirement is planned for the shorthaired pointer that won Westminster. If she's considering a second career, maybe she should talk to my dog. She's been around the block a few times—just today, as a matter of fact—and when it comes to careers, she's got some advice: It's a tough world out there, and you don't get treats just for showing up. Watch out for wheelchairs, and when dealing with cows, always—ALWAYS—have backup.

June 9, 2005

At Least She's Not a Large White Rabbit

The dog ponders a question concerning waterfowl.

LATELY I'VE BEEN receiving some strange looks when I take the dog for a walk. Maybe it's because I'm one of those people who talk to their dogs.

It's all fairly normal, though, similar to any conversation you'd have with a four year old: "Come on, let's go to the woods." "No, not those woods, the new woods." "That's a duck. They don't bite." "That's a swan; they spit." "A Bewicks swan...why, does it matter?"

Not at all like the man I overheard in Sam's Club one day, having a serious conversation with the Kikkoman's.

I've been thinking of teaching her sign language, but throwing signs to a dog might also be construed as weird, or downright anti-social, for which they have ASBOs here, or anti-social behaviour orders. Personally, I can't think of anything more social than talking to your dog, but this is a country where the government limits the size of stuffed animals, yet looks the other way when people drive 159 mph, the speed at which an off-duty patrol car was recently clocked.

They also have signs everywhere that say "Keep Your Dog on a Lead," which I scrupulously obeyed, until I noticed no one else did. There were dogs running loose all over Regent's Park, packs of them: big dogs, little dogs, dogs with spots, dogs with hats, dogs Dr. Seuss hadn't even imagined.

One day I heard a little boy ask his dad, "What does that sign say?"

"Keep. Your. Dog. On. A. Lead," the father read.

"What's a lead?" the little boy asked. As the father patiently ex-plained, several dogs milled around, none encumbered by leads. I knew what was coming next, but no, even the little boy understood the gray areas of the English law better than I.

As I said to my dog just the other day, "It's amazing to think our common law actually derived from the British system, as many dif-ferences as there are, particularly when it comes to interpreting the impact of various social legislation."

She seemed to agree, although some days, you'd think I was just talking to the soy sauce.

October 10, 2005

A Day At Dunstable Downs, With Dog

The dog waits at a kissing gate.

YESTERDAY WAS A FINE October day, the perfect day for a hike, or a ramble, as the English call a long walk over the countryside (preferably accompanied by a dog). The law gives the public right of way over privately owned land, a concept that would be greeted with gunfire in America. Armed with a guidebook of "circular walks through history," we drove to Dunstable Downs in Bedfordshire, where the English apparently go to fly their kites. There were kiteists out in force, dozens of them guiding their kites expertly through the currents.

We'd also stumbled onto a hotbed of glider activity. The wind off the ridge must be just right for gliding. Some were taking off via a pulley system that towed them almost vertically up and then released them into the atmosphere—a stomach-clenching performance. Others were towed by prop planes, which rather defeats the purpose.

The dog soon grew bored watching the gliders, so we took off, peering into the guidebook for instructions. They led us along the Icknield Way, first trod thousands of years ago by Neolithic Man. The first M-road, used for marketing the high quality flint produced in the region.

Nowadays, the neoliths have been replaced by sheep. In addition to their wool, sheep create a by-product which my dog considers a tasty tidbit. (And yes, I'm one of those people who kiss their dogs. But the memory will have to fade before I allow my lips to touch hers. Call me finicky.) Conscious of her dignity in front of the sheep, we leashed her anyway, after she ignored our warning: "Do not eat shit! And no, I'm not speaking metaphorically of rubbish in general, that really is shit!" (Too wordy?)

Her reply: A shit-eating grin. (Score: Dog, 1)

Soon we came to the Tree Cathedral, planted by Edmund Blyth after the First World War to honor his wartime comrades. The site, a former chicken run, is probably the only cathedral that changes color in the fall. I'm glad we saw it in the fall—the rhododendrons in springtime are surely too cheeky. We rested here, drank in the beauty of the season, and watched the dog romp in the cloister. (A first for her.)

Our private service over, we hiked to the next marker, a pub in Whipsnade Heath with a well-trimmed thatched roof (one of over 100,000 thatched roofs in England). The 15th-century Old Hunters Lodge looked inviting, until I realized the décor, as well as the menu, was probably from the Early Hunter-Gatherer period. Not my taste at all.

Past the heath we scrambled up an almost vertical incline, and I saw why having four feet might be an advantage. Then on to a kissing gate, and the dog saw why having two arms might be an advantage. (Score: tied.)

The trail circled Kensworth quarry, first mined 4000 years ago by Neoliths digging for flint. Alternating lines of chalk and rock lie exposed on its face, giving away its age. The Neoliths here have been replaced by huge digging machines, carting away 800 tons an hour, but they were silent on a Sunday.

Back at the Downs, kites still dove and rippled in the late afternoon sun, but the gliders had all retreated to the pub. Satisfied with a few nuts I'd packed and the blackberries we'd filched along the way, we hopped in the car, filthy and tired.

On the way home, the dog tossed her, uh, cookies all over the back seat. She sheepishly admitted sheep droppings probably weren't a good idea. "At least on an empty stomach," she added, looking hopefully at my peanuts.

(Victory: Humans.)

March 1, 2006

The Curious Incident Involving Tony Blair's Squirrel

Chequers, scene of the crime incident.

WE HIKED AROUND Chequers today, which is the prime minister's country residence, the equivalent of Camp David, for my American-based readers. Except it's not nearly so well guarded; there's basically a sign saying "Private, No Admittance" and some really large cameras that will shoot any intruder.

Anyway, in the wood next to the estate, my dog was involved in an incident, as we are calling it. I've talked to those who witnessed it and they all say that basically the squirrel just ran into her mouth. There was no chasing involved. They are quite certain of this. And when I told her to drop it, she did so immediately, placing it gently on to the ground, obviously quite concerned about the welfare of this poor misguided rodent that jumped into her mouth.

She actually seemed rather bemused by the whole thing. All these years chasing the damn things, and there's one just here for the taking?! What gives?

I'm sure if the incident was caught on camera my version of events will be backed up. After hiking a mile or more uphill, my dog was in no condition to actually assault a swift-footed squirrel, even one that was clearly leading her on. (Someone thought they heard a little squirrel voice squealing "come and get me, bitch!")

So then someone's cellphone rang. "It's Tony Blair; he wants his squirrel back."

(Sorry; rambler humor.)

It was suggested that the squirrel could have had bird flu, which was discovered in a cat in Germany. Maybe. But so far no bird flu has been detected in Britain, and the squirrel didn't look as if it had been vacationing on the continent.

If bird flu has arrived, Tony Blair will be the first to know. Anyone got a number for him? Maybe I'll ring him up; explain how the whole thing happened, get the latest on the bird flu situation. And tell him he might want to keep an eye on those squirrels in his wood; they are acting a bit strange.

August 28, 2006

A Visit to Verulamium

The dog makes another important archaeological discovery.

YESTERDAY WE WENT to Verulamium, an ancient Roman city that was sacked by Queen Boudicca. Verulamium was a crown jewel of the Roman empire in Britain. You may know it today as St Albans, a crown jewel in the Starbucks empire.

We took the dog to the park there, and she ran ahead as usual. She was the first to discover the remains of the Roman city wall. She was hoping they'd left some bones, but no such luck.

She asked me what happened to the Roman empire. I told her they were brought down by hubris. She asked if she should be vaccinated against that, but I told her it only seems to affect humans.

August 2, 2007

Close Encounters With Mrs. Tiggy-Winkle

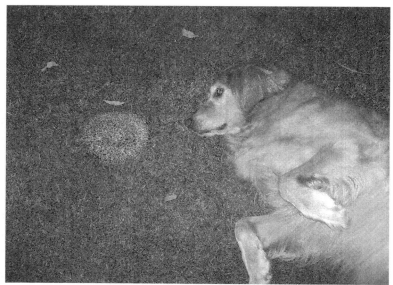

"Hey Mom, look who came to play with me!"

LATE LAST NIGHT we let the dog out, and she promptly alerted us with a bark: "Nighttime intruders! Reinforcements needed!"

So Daughter Number Two and I armed ourselves with a flashlight and went to see how we could help. There's been a fox coming round lately, nosing in the compost, and we hoped she or he had come back. Or maybe it was one of the muntjac deer that populate Buckinghamshire.

But instead we found the dog was trying to befriend the hedgehog again. Mrs. Tiggy-Winkle has told her in no uncertain terms that a relationship is out of the question, but my dog insists on trying to reach out. (She's had a bad reputation in this county, ever since she nicked one of Tony Blair's squirrels. The smaller mammal species steer well clear of her.)

I grabbed my camera and my daughter, who wants to befriend the hedgehog almost as much as the dog, mustered up the courage to pet Mrs. Tiggy-Winkle. She spotted a slug nearby, and when I told her that's what hedgehogs eat, she mustered up even more courage and picked it up, placing it gingerly near what she assumed was the mouth end of Mrs. T. We hoped it would be interpreted as a sign that we natives were friendly, or at least that our yard has good grub.

Did I mention that my daughters both had Beatrix Potter bedding when they were infants? And the complete set of Peter Rabbit dinnerware, as well as the books? We like the idea of having hedgehogs in our garden, almost as much as we like having cows next door.

But this was not the charming vermin-infested garden of Beatrix Potter. Poor Mrs. T. probably was imagining she'd happened upon a scene from *Close Encounters of the Third Kind*, as I snapped photos with my flash while DNT held the flashlight.

Then the dog had a go at peace negotiations. She lay down right next to her, having heard something about lions lying down with lambs. She looked longingly toward Mrs. Tiggy-Winkle, but hedgehogs have very prickly temperaments. Mrs. T. refused to budge an inch, not exhibiting the least bit of curiosity about another species.

We don't get the slugs out for just anyone, I tell you, so after that we called the dog in, turned out the light, and finished watching our movie.

Beatrix Potter must have had a different sort of hedgehog in her garden.

July 31, 2008

Campaign '08: The Dog Runs for Local Council

Vote for my dog. She'll keep you safe from terrorist squirrels.

IN ALABAMA, a dog is running for mayor. In Alaska, a dog has run for governor, losing by a nose. (A rather long nose, as it turns out.)

Not to be outdone, my dog has decided to throw her hat—err, collar—in the ring as well. (If you know anything about my dog, you know she pretty much lives for attention, and she sees how much attention we pay to politicians around here.)

Plus, politicians get lots of treats, and she wants a piece of that action. So she's decided to run. Not for mayor—that's a ceremonial position here, one you have to be bred for. No, she figures she'll be most effective serving on the Local Council.

She's got a pretty good platform which, as her communications director, I've cleaned up a bit. (Spelling is not her strong point.)

My Dog, On the Issues:

Community:

- Expand the Common, providing more shady paths for hot summer days, and a bigger pond for spontaneous dips.
- Make the playground more dog friendly by increasing the number of picnic tables.

"Picnic tables and appropriately-sized playground equipment will assist in making dogs more agile."

Rubbish:

- Rubbish collection shall be every day, since bags of rotting rubbish add beauty to our neighbourhoods.
- Place more dog waste bins in the Common. This will prevent the need for anti-social behaviour.
- On the other hand, there are far too many rubbish bins in our community, taking up valuable space that could be filled with interesting litter.

"It's nice when people toss their litter right on the pavement. Large buns from the cafe are especially a welcome scent."

Commerce:

- Shops should be prohibited from banning dogs. This includes the library.
- The Fun Fair should be held every weekend, as candy floss will attract the right sorts.
- We should encourage more restaurants to open up in this community.

"All those lovely frying smells improve the quality of life for a community's residents."

Crime:

- Burglary is a community-wide problem. Dogs should be given free rein to patrol their neighbourhoods at night, and barking at scary-looking strangers will be encouraged. People who complain about this will be politely told to bugger off.

- In the interest of diversity, nice, peace-loving cats will be welcome in our community. Aggressive cats shall be put on notice that we will not tolerate anti-social behaviour such as spitting or hissing.
- Hedgehogs should also be encouraged to relocate to our community, after first passing Good Citizen tests. Like knife crime, offenses involving quills will be prosecuted fully.
- Male dogs who've been declared sexual predators should be castrated, and leashed at all times.

"I have been tough on crime my entire life, as my neighbours will testify."

Testimonial: "Can't you make that damned dog shut up?"

Roads:

- Speed limits should be lowered and strictly enforced. Large scary lorries should be banned from residential areas, no matter where their sat navs direct them to go.
- Parking rules should be enforced, with exceptions for disabled pets.
- Our streets need more safe crosswalks, with the button at paw level.

"Every dog should be able to reach crosswalk buttons, to ensure equal opportunity for tiny terriers as well as large Labradors to run across the street after squirrels."

Discrimination:

- Dogs of all colour and creed should be allowed free and unfettered access to our community. (However, spotted dogs, due to their aggressive nature, must remain on leads.)
- Asylum-seeking dogs (such as those from the Dalmation coast) should learn English with the help of such community classes as "Language for the Restaurant."

• No more glass ceilings.

"Bitches should enjoy the same rights as male dogs and be free from harassment in the work, err, walking place."

Taxes:

• Humans should be expected to pay their fair share, and when a dog performs an endearing trick, treats must be paid immediately. Therefore, all humans will be required to carry treats in a convenient waist pack.

• Taxation according to one's income: High Value Treats from those who can afford them.

"An adequate supply of treats are essential to a well run society."

Terrorism:

• Cells of terrorist squirrels are known to train in this area. They will be chased relentlessly on an as-needed basis.

Experience:

• Experience interacting with the local Animal Warden.

• Lived and traveled on multiple continents, maintaining a current Pet Passport.

• Thoroughly vetted.

You may contribute to the campaign here: dogstrust.co.uk.

CHAPTER EIGHT

Nature

England is beautiful, for six months of the year anyway. I discovered a latent passion for flowers of all kinds: weeds, cultivated roses, and even crops.

June 4, 2005

Greys Court: Winding Wisteria, a Haha, and an Amazing Labyrinth

Wisteria pergola at Greys Court

I LOVE ENGLAND. Really, I do, and I'd like you to remind me in December, when the days are short and damp and cold, that spring is worth every minute of winter. The English are simply the best gardeners on earth, and in springtime this island reaps a floral bounty that would turn God herself green with envy.

Gardening was never a passion of mine. I liked flowers all right, but driving an hour to look at a garden...what folly!

Trust me, these gardens are worth it.

Today we went to Greys Court, near Henley-on-Thames. I went specifically to see the 100-year-old wisteria pergola I'd read about in the National Trust gardening magazine. (Yep, I've even started reading gardening magazines.) If anything typifies the English garden, it's wisteria. Graceful purple flowers (racemes) drape elegantly from tenacious vines, clinging to walls and pergolas as if by super glue.

The wisteria at Greys Court has settled in for the long haul, and hardly needs its wooden support beams. I was afraid its blooms would be played out by now, but the dark sheltered pergola means a slightly later blooming season, so the flowers still dangled above our heads as we walked through the arched bower.

The wisteria, of course, is only part of the charms found at Greys Court. With dumb luck we arrived on the first Saturday of the month, when the house was also open for visits. Like many English houses, its history isn't fully known, but it has been continuously occupied since the 14th century. One previous owner added plasterwork on the drawing room wall, a three-dimensional floral design reminiscent of Wedgewood. (No photos allowed, sorry.) The home is now owned by the National Trust and occupied by the son of the last owners, the Brunner family.

A series of walled gardens, cared for by three full time gardeners, are filled with roses, peonies, clematis, and dozens of other blooms I didn't recognize. The kitchen garden was large enough to stock the Waitrose produce section, but somehow artichokes look much lovelier in their natural habitat than in supermarket bins.

The labyrinth (they call it a "maze") invited us to trace its quarter mile of brick paths, but the rhododendron bower at its edge proved even more alluring. Memories of playing beneath the azalea bushes when I was young made me wish I was still five and didn't have to drive home later.

We wandered along the haha (a steep-sided ditch used to pen livestock instead of a view-obstructing wall), crossed the Moon

Bridge, and discovered the thatched ice house, rebuilt over a 15-foot deep brick shaft.

I suppose after a few more years I'll be more blasé about gardens such as these. ("Another clematis arch? Yawn.") After all, I lived in New Mexico five years and hardly turned an eye toward the mountains' majesty after a few seasons.

But I hope not. After all, there are hundreds more gardens to explore, and I've just learned how to spell "Ceanothus."

May 22, 2006

When I Am Old I Shall Grow Purple Flowers

Wisteria wanna-bes

I'VE BEEN TAKING photos of flowers the last week or so. Many are of the wisteria that climbs up the walls of many houses here in the Chilterns. (If you prefer roses and dahlias, you'll have to wait a while.)

I think I'll write a book called The Wisteria Hunter. Maybe Meryl Streep will play me in the movie....

Purple and blue flowers seem to be my favorite. The lilacs here are also blooming. They seem exotic to me, since when I was growing up in the American South I never saw one. We had redbuds aplenty, and dogwood and azaleas, but when I was given the book *Under the Lilacs* by Louisa May Alcott I couldn't imagine what they looked like. Then I moved to Ohio and we had boring white lilacs.

What's the point? Lilacs should at least make the effort.

One day I'll have a garden full of purple lilacs, bluebells, and wisteria.

And I shall wear purple too.

June 5, 2006

Where Have All the Flowers Gone?

THE OTHER DAY I asked my gardener what these pretty yellow flowers were. "Weeds," he told me.

"But those blue ones? Surely they're not weeds..."

Yes, they're weeds too. In fact, whenever I ask about anything coming up in my garden, the answer is usually the same. Although I would call them wildflowers instead of weeds.

Forget-me-nots, bluebells, poppies, daisies, cow parsley, and whatever these yellow flowers are called, grow in wild abandon here, along the roadsides, in the woodlands, in pastures, in my shady garden.

I wondered, why is it the only wildflowers I can identify are dandelions? I've lived around the United States—South, North, East, and West, and I've never noticed such a variety of wildflowers, i.e. weeds, before.

Maybe it's because in the US we've eradicated them. Those herbicides that keep our lawns spotless and our crops free of Johnson grass also take out the wildflowers. Over time this has to have had an effect, despite the best efforts of wildflower enthusiasts like Lady Bird Johnson. I don't think herbicides are used as frequently over here, in fact the EU has banned quite a few of our favorites.

So maybe that's why I've got all these lovely weeds popping up in my garden. I like them; they come up every year with no prompting on my part. Unfortunately, the stinging nettle comes up too, in amongst the blackberries.

I guess you have to take the nettles along with the flowers.

September 17, 2006

A Walk, By Any Other Name

The Watlington "white mark"

I DON'T THINK I've explained the concept of "a walk" before; that is, exactly what British people mean when they say they're going for a walk. Chances are they don't intend a leisurely stroll around the 'hood. To the English, fond of understatement, a walk is what an American, fond of overstatement, would call a hike.

Walks are big business here. There are Ramblers Associations (a walk is also called a ramble, by more serious walkers) and websites aimed at devotees. Bookstores have shelves of books dedicated to circular walks in every region of the English countryside. I have several books featuring walks around the Chilterns, and no two are the same. The hardest part (other than climbing the steep Chiltern hills) is deciding which one to take on a beautiful September Sunday.

The walks typically start at a pub or public carpark, and continue through woods, over pastures, along rivers, down ancient "roads," up and down hills, and across village lanes—all in one walk. With most of Britain's land open by law to public access, there are very few places that aren't networked by well-marked public footpaths.

The walks are almost always dog friendly, but you are expected to keep your dog under control, and on a lead when near livestock, especially during lambing season. The kissing gates and stiles are designed with dogs in mind—there is always room for even a retriever to scoot underneath. Only once have I had to heave her over a stile that was missing a "portcullis" entry for dogs.

An average walk is from 4-10 miles in length, but one must make allowances for the inevitable missteps. The directions, which seem so clear at first glance, often make no sense at all when the countryside looms: is this the clearing referred to, or is it further down? And what's a copse, anyway?

On the walk we took today, near Watlington, the directions said "with the White Mark to the left, follow the trail down the hill." Only problem, we didn't see the White Mark, or in fact know what the White Mark was (having failed to do the proper research beforehand). So we wandered around a bit, following other trails, until we backtracked and saw an unmistakable chalk carving in the hillside.

The White Mark was carved in 1784 by Edward Horner, who thought the village church should have a spire that could be seen from miles away. So he carved one in the hillside. (There are a lot of chalk hill figures, mostly horses, in Southern England, the oldest being the Uffington White Horse near Oxford.)

We managed to find the section of the walk that went along the Icknield Way—after all, the oldest path in Britain is hard to miss. But we made a mistake again when we went right instead of left on path

W6. No problem; this way allowed us to walk near a lovely herd of cows.

We went down One Tree Hill, named for the ancient yew tree that once stood all alone on the hillside. Now there's a replacement yew, protected by a fence.

The views were spectacular, just like the description of the walk said. Rolling green hills in every direction, the village of Watlington nestled below as if posing for a postcard. In fact, the views are so great the escarpment was once used for a line of beacons to warn of the approaching Spanish Armada.

If you're interested in another walk that we took along the Icknield Way, be sure to read about our hike last year along Dunstable Downs.

See how in that last sentence I typed "hike"? I am, after all, still an American fond of overstatement.

April 30, 2007

Follow the Yellow Brick...Field?

Field of rape in Oxfordshire

IT'S NOT MY IMAGINATION: this year, there is more rape covering England than ever before. Everywhere I go—into East Anglia last week, to the Midlands on Saturday, and through Oxfordshire today, I see field after field glowing florescent yellow, bright as a highlighter marker on a once-green page. The pungent odor, the scent of sweaty old ladies, wafts in through car windows, making you wonder which of your companions forgot to bathe.

Farmers are planting rapeseed, known in America as canola, not because the country has suddenly developed a taste for the healthy cooking oil, but because rapeseed oil is now used for biofuels. I read a headline that predicted beer drinkers would protest when they realized the cost of beer had gone up, due to barley fields being turned over to rape.

You won't find rape in any quaint Victorian paintings. You won't read of rape farmers in Thomas Hardy's novels, or in Betjeman's poems. Rape, a relative of mustard, used to contain toxic levels of erucic acid, until the wily Canadians figured out how to cross breed plants that contained healthful oleic acid instead of erucic acid (and then rebranded it as canola oil) sometime in the 1970s. Better yet, canola oil contains mono-unsaturated fat as well as omega-3, making it one of the healthiest cooking oils around.

Sadly, despite the omnipresence of rape plants (brassica napus) in southern England, it is still a relatively rare sight on supermarket shelves. (Tesco does carry an organic brand at some of their stores.)

Aside from its health benefits, rape is one of the most beautiful crops around. I love to see it highlighting the countryside, though I've heard some people complain that it's a garish sight. But I love to round a curve and see fields of bright yellow, pieced together by green hedgerows.

This year rape is blooming about a month earlier than usual, as are all our spring blossoms. (We've just finished up the hottest April since records began in the 17th century.) I don't know if fueling our cars with rapeseed oil is the answer, but it sure makes me want to get out and enjoy the countryside.

Fortunately, I'm not allergic to rape. If you are, you might want to avoid England in April and May.

October 8, 2007

Chenies: Host to Kings, Queens, and Now, Me

The front of Chenies Manor, built in the mid-fifteenth century.

I'VE HIKED PAST Chenies Manor House four times, peering through the garden walls, yet never returned for a visit during the hours they were open. So, one afternoon last week, I decided it was high time I did.

Now, I've been to dozens of stately homes, National Trust properties, castles, palaces, and proper British cottages, but I have to admit I was not too jaded to enjoy Chenies. First of all, it's very old. There's been a residence here since the Domesday Book of 1086, and even before that, in Saxon times. Second, quite a few people who even I recognize have stayed here: Edward I, Henry VIII, Anne Boleyn, and Elizabeth I—who visited as an infant and again as monarch.

You can trod upon the old oak floors in the very room where she worked, and with very little effort, imagine yourself a member of her court.

Chenies also has the distinction of being one of the houses where Catherine Howard, Henry's fifth wife, engaged in the adultery that eventually got her killed. In fact, it's said to be haunted, perhaps by Henry VIII himself.

This home, unlike many others in Stately Britain, is still lived in, and has an air of pragmatic stateliness. It's been used as a location for many films, including a BBC special on Jane Austen. (A couple of the rooms had been repainted blue for the program.) It's a great place to see antiques and tapestries in situ, including several pieces from the 16th century. The billiard table is large enough to field a cricket team—fortunately, the floor was reinforced or I'd never have dared to go back downstairs.

You can count the 22 cut brick chimneys—built by the same man who built the chimneys at Hampton Court Palace. There's a tunnel, in case the family need to escape quickly, and a little room to hide a priest, should the need ever arise.

The gardens, even in the early days of October, were stunning. A pink garden, a topiary garden, a maze, a physic garden (don't touch!) were all blooming along as if summer were still at full strength. The kitchen garden was awash in chard, shallots, and other fall veggies.

The manor house is open two afternoons a week from April to October, and is located a short bus ride from the Chorleywood Tube station. It's worth a visit, something I wish I'd known the first time I walked past and wondered what was behind those walls.

May 14, 2008

Wisteria: The Competition Intensifies

Cascading wisteria racemes

A FRIEND CALLED last night: "What are you doing?"

I swallowed my focaccia. "Just finished eating," I said. "Why?"

"Let's go look at wisteria," she replied.

What does it say about me that, not only am I the type of person who'll drop everything to go to a sleepy village just to look at wisteria, but that my friends know that I'm that type of person?

It turned out to be a great idea. The village of Denham is just inside the M25, yet you'd think you were in the deepest, twee-ist heart of England, it's so lovely. Of course, a large part of that loveliness is due to the ancient wisteria vines that stretch across aged brick cottages, each wall competing for Best Wisteria Vine Ever.

We were drunk with the scent of wisteria before we ever got to the pub.

My friend, who'd earlier tried to convince me the wisteria in Denham was the best, was right. Or spot on, as they say...see for yourself:

St Mary's churchyard

Wisteria peeks over into the churchyard, where grave stones have been moved and lined up against the fence. (Health and Safety strikes again.)

The cottage on the end was once the home of the actor Sir John Mills.

It goes on and on and on...down one side of the street, and up the other.

This man is probably a judge from the Wisteria Society. Or maybe he just wants to go to the popular public house, The Swan.

August 3, 2010

Hampstead Heath, London's Lungs

Hampstead Heath—no, not a Monet

ON SATURDAY I PAID my first visit to Hampstead Heath in London. Despite having been told many times how delightful it is, especially for walkers, I'd never been. But a friend suggested we visit Kenwood House, which overlooks the Heath. It's a bit hard to get to—it's a mile from the nearest Tube, then a 20 minute walk or a 20 minute bus ride. And the nearest Tube happens to be a 25-minute train ride plus three Tube exchanges for me.

When I was living in London during my first month here, people would recommend Hampstead Heath as a great dog walking spot, but sadly, we never figured out a way to get the dog there. By the time we had a car, we lived so near to other great walks there didn't seem to be a reason to head into town just for a good walk.

But Hampstead Heath is about more than walking. The views are magnificent, too, especially from Parliament Hill, where kites fly year round. The London skyline to the south is punctuated by St Paul's Cathedral and the Swiss Re building—the Gherkin.

And then there's the English Heritage property Kenwood House, full of priceless artwork, including a Vermeer, a Rembrandt, and so many portraits by Sir Joshua Reynolds, landscapes by Constable, and charming animal portraits by Landseer, you'd think you were in the Tate Britain.

Kenwood House is a typical Palladian-style pile, remodeled by the architect Robert Adam. Entry is free, due to a bequest by Lord Iveagh, who left it in the care of English Heritage upon his death in 1927. (Donations are welcome, however.) On weekends music concerts take place on the grounds, which apparently annoyed the neighbors in leafy Hampstead. (I know how they feel.)

It was because of an upcoming concert that much of the grounds were roped off, so I couldn't get a photo from a proper distance. However, if you saw the film *Notting Hill*, you saw the house—it was the scene of Julia Roberts' period film, where poor Hugh Grant learned he'd been played for a fool.

Hampstead Heath is known as the "lungs of London," though these days the air of London isn't quite as polluted as it once was (thank the congestion charge for that!). There are several ponds, some of them suitable for swimming (including Ladies Only, Men Only, and Mixed), and plenty of paths, some of them suitable for cycling.

Sometimes I forget how wonderful it is to live so near to London. But trudging up Hampstead Heath on a hot July afternoon reminds me right quick.

CHAPTER NINE

Visits to the Home Country

After living in England for several years, I found a
visit to the United States brought new insights.

May 12, 2006

Reasons the Boston Tea Party Should Never Have Happened

SOME THINGS I missed while I was gone:

My luggage. Once again American Airlines lost my luggage, but at least it showed up the next day (instead of the three days it took last time). I was much calmer this time round, probably because I know the secret word to talk to an agent instead of a recording.

Talk radio. Yes, I know there's talk radio in the states. But it's not anything like BBC Radio 4. Not even NPR comes close. No Desert Island Disks is like, well, living on a desert island.

Speed cameras. You can almost always avoid them, which means you can ignore the speed limits 99% of the time. Like a true New Mexican, I tend to think certain laws don't apply to me, including the 70-mph speed limit on near deserted interstates. (No, I didn't get a ticket. I would have talked myself out of it, citing a national emergency or at least a hair appointment.)

Proper tea. I brought my own tea, but when I asked for hot water at the hotel I got a Styrofoam cup of boiling water. There is a certain lack of civilization to this method of tea drinking. It's almost as bad as putting ice in perfectly good tea.

Flowers. They are everywhere in England, on the verges, in tiny gardens, on old graves, in crowded city centres. Even petrol stations sell bunches of fresh flowers. Possibly that's to cushion the blow of our higher gas prices. (Currently a litre of petrol is just under a pound here. Do the maths.)

Good bread. Again, those service stations here sell a variety of bread, including ciabatta, pita, and wholemeal. The only thing Chevron offered was a loaf of white Holsom. I decided notebook paper would be a healthier option.

On the other hand, I was driving a Chevrolet Uplander, since I had to move my mom. My god, your parking spaces are huge! Each one had plenty of room for my behemoth and a few Minis.

I managed to avoid fast food, the scourge of America, but I can't say I never stepped foot in chain restaurants, another, albeit lesser, scourge. In Baton Rouge I met a friend at P.F. Chang's, a pan-Asian chain that transcends the chain restaurant genre characterized by Bennigan's and Applebee's.

Try their eggplant. It almost made up for the lack of proper tea elsewhere.

December 13, 2006

Home Again

OBSERVATIONS FROM MY TRIP to Vegetarian Hell, known otherwise as the Deep South:

The entire country has gone to the dogs. Honestly, what is it with the designer dog clothes at Target and elsewhere? I can get both casual wear and formal wear for my dog, jewelry, gourmet dog treats, designer label pet carriers, and Shabby Chic chew toys if I were the type of person to spoil my dog. All right, I *am* the type of person to spoil my dog but the day I start dressing her is the day you should put me in a long-term care facility.

The Dallas airport has no vegan food. I finally found a veggie burger at Bennigan's, of all places. Normally I don't eat in airports, but I was there for five hours. Someone should open a healthy restaurant in Terminal D.

On the other hand, the veggie meals on American Airlines are very good. I even asked for a recipe.

I ate three spinach salads while I was gone, which usually was the closest thing to vegan on the menu. And when I say "leave off the cheese" I am talking about mozzarella, which is still classified as "cheese" despite the presence of god-knows-what.

The electricity went out at my in-laws' house after a massive storm system moved through. When it rains in Louisiana, it really pours.

It was colder in the Deep South than it was in England, which is really weird. I like to've froze.

Southern grammar has a way of sneaking up on you, but I have not yet uttered the phrase "she don't want no fried chicken" although it is tempting.

Nursing homes are dominated by females. Almost all the patients are women, and all but a couple of employees are female too. When a man walks in all eyes turn toward him. He's usually carrying a Bible.

Women traveling alone are ignored by female flight attendants, and doted on by male flight attendants. (But I don't normally answer to "sweetie." Trust me.) Airport lounges are also the province of men, and when I walked in the attendant assumed I was with the man ahead of me.

It took three Target employees to find the DVD of *An Inconvenient Truth* which the first two had not heard of. Now I know why they call it an inconvenient truth.

Target also has vegan boots for $24. That's only £12! I quickly tossed a pair of size 8s into my shopping cart in case someone else had their eye on them, but I bet I needn't have worried. Probably no one else knows how much vegan boots cost at Stella McCartney's shop in Mayfair.

There is just way too much stuff available in American shops, in addition to designer doggie wear. But I didn't see a whole lot of people out buying it. Which was fine with me, because I needed to shop for certain things I can't get here, or can't get economically here, including a hair cut. My daughter says it looks very "L.A." but I think she meant "Louisiana."

I only drove on the wrong side of the road once, on a stretch of deserted highway near St Francisville, when I backtracked to take a photo of a cow.

Cows in Louisiana are not as friendly. I'm sure that's related to the fact that there is a scarcity of vegetarian meals.

February 18, 2009

Impressions of the Southern United States

SOMETIMES I THINK the main reason to have a blog is to have a place to complain when things annoy me. Facebook status updates don't do justice to certain outrageousness, you know what I mean?

While in the US recently I was annoyed by a lot of things, but I don't want to sound like I complain too much, so I'll list the things I like first.

Some things I like about the US, the South in particular:

1. Yellow squash. Can't get enough of it, and it's impossible to find here. (It figures, my number one item would be food.)

2. Lipton Pyramid Green Tea. (Yes, the number two item is also ingestible.)

3. Warmth. Warm water coming straight from the tap. Makes hand washing nicer.

4. Chipotles. If not for the food, would I ever return?

5. Big parking spaces. Nice for food shopping.

6. Paper towels in public restrooms (not called toilets, I was reminded). Except for the new high speed hand dryers at certain train stations, the whoosh of air we get in England just doesn't cut it.

7. Friendliness. It amazes me that folks are willing to talk to strangers without a dog nearby. (In England folks are quite friendly if you're walking a dog.) I had several conversations in the produce section of Wal-Mart.

8. Family. It gets harder and harder to say goodbye.

Things I hate about the US, the South in particular:

1. TV. I'd forgotten how inane television is in the US, now that "The West Wing" is no longer shown. The "talking head" style of news coverage is particularly stupefying. See:

2. Nancy Grace. God I hate that woman.

3. Physicians who think they're gods. And refuse to divulge their information to mere mortals, i.e. patients. "You sit down and we shine a light in your eyes" is not a proper description of a surgical procedure.

4. Bugs. Giant cockroaches. Little cockroaches. And the need to kill them with strong chemicals.

5. No green grass in the winter. Our grass is green in England, despite a week of snow before I left. I love me some green grass.

6. Giant American cars. Couldn't believe some of the monstrosities, still on the road after decades. (And yes, I'm aware this conflicts with number 5, above. I'm a mess of contradictions.)

7. Poverty. Living in Northern Europe, one forgets there is such abject poverty amidst the wealth of America.

8. Southern accents. "Drops" does not have four syllables. (Okay, that one cracked me up when the nurse said it. Fortunately she wasn't paying attention to me.)

9. Fast food. Competing scents from various hamburger joints are overwhelming at certain times of the day.

10. Traffic signals. Busy roads have dozens, at every parking lot entrance, minor intersection, etc. They make driving harrowing, I imagine, for European visitors used to sliding in and out of roundabouts.

11. No public transport. For my daughter, who can't drive until her eye is healed, it's inconceivable that there's no public transportation to her school.

12. No circular walks. People in England know what I'm talking about. Sadly, we went to a lovely lakeside park on a beautiful Sunday

and found it deserted. The trail we took ended after two miles, forcing us to retrace our steps. How odd.

13. Preoccupation with missing white girls. See number 2. What is it with wall-to-wall coverage of people's anguish and dysfunctional families?

14. Bad grammar. Just stop it with the double negatives. And especially stop it while talking loudly on your cell phone.

15. Dogs that run loose. I don't mean at public parks, but in neighborhoods. Scared me to death when two dogs came up to me, barking, while I took a walk. (I realized that this would not scare me at all in England. Dogs are just different here.)

16. Certain food items. Did you know you can buy brains in a can? This can't be healthy.

There. I got it all out.

November 21, 2011

Oh Beautiful, For Spacious Aisles

I'M OFF TO THE US tomorrow, and I'm trying to prepare myself for the culture shock. Most people can't understand why I find things other Americans take for granted, like driving on the right side of the road, so odd. But after seven years abroad, I feel more like an alien in my home country than a natural born citizen.

It's not so much the speech, though I'm shocked when Southerners take four syllables to pronounce what is otherwise a single-syllable word. I still speak American English like a native, albeit one who has an odd way with "water" and "butter."

Rather, it's the day-to-day getting around that I find alternately baffling, frustrating, or simply amazing.

Those amber waves of grain have been mowed and turned into huge parking lots—some of which are meant to be roads. But they no longer function as such, due to the many impediments placed in the way of the driver.

Take traffic lights, a ubiquitous feature of US roadways. God shed his grace on America along with thousands of miles of concrete, and then crowned it all with multicolored traffic lights—which don't have the good sense to turn yellow before going green the way they do in the UK.

The few traffic lights in Britain are mostly for pedestrian crossings rather than intersections. My small town just added two new pedestrian crossings when the new Tesco opened, which drivers found a huge impediment and pedestrians, who were used to dashing across the high street, found equally annoying.

Which is another odd thing: shopping in the UK is mostly done on the "high street" which is sort of like Main Street in the US, only it's not a concept, it's an actual street. It may not be named "High Street," although often it is, but it's the main road in a town where most commerce takes place. (Our high street is actually named Packhorse, a common street name here. Other roads are named for where they go, which means London Road and Oxford Road are, naturally, the same road.)

Shopping in the US, on the other hand, most often takes place at or near a mall. Surrounding a mall are dozens of large and small stores, connected by a system of super-sized carparks requiring an advanced global positioning system just to navigate. It reminds me of a giant pinball machine, with your oversized car the pinball, searching desperately to find its way out of the maze. Or at least to the empty parking space nearest to Target's red front doors.

And Target—is there any place more beloved than Target? Even Michelle Obama was recently spotted pushing a red shopping cart (with its wheels spinning in only one direction, mind you!) through the wide, spotless aisles of TargGHAY, as Americans ironically refer to the upscale discount superstore. How many times have I walked into Target, intending to buy one thing, and I come out $200 later with a shopping cart full of cheap t-shirts and polka dot serving bowls and a rug to match?

It's like every high street shop, combined into one giant red bullseye. With free parking!

I am convinced the main reason I hate to shop in the UK is the lack of convenient parking. I willingly walk miles every day for pleasure, but when I'm shopping I can't bear the idea of parking a quarter mile from the shops and dragging purchases back to my cramped car in its too small parking space. Opening the car door without hitting another car is like performing delicate surgery in a toilet. (Which of course is never said in America, unless you sell plumbing fixtures. Americans go to the "bathroom" or the "restroom" though many women go to the "little girls' room.")

Most amazing of all, though, is that at most large American stores you can shop 24/7! (A term Americans invented to describe the proper functioning of commerce.) That includes Sunday, since blue laws, in the spirit of unbridled consumerism, were abolished ages ago. Even chain bookstores like Barnes and Noble are open until eleven p.m. But I like to go early, when I'm wide awake at five, due to the time difference. Those aisles at the superstores are even wider then, and I can wheel my ungainly shopping cart unhindered through corridors freshly stocked with a fabulous array of items. I find things I never knew I needed, and almost never regret purchasing. Like socks. Polka dot socks, to match the throw rug and the serving bowl.

And when I pay for my purchases, I can slide my non-chip and pin debit card through a little machine myself, punch the proper buttons, and never hand it over to anyone else! Likewise, it's easy to get more cash: drive-through ATMs are everywhere. It's like scoring extra points by hitting the right bumper in the pinball game, except you score some extra cash when you drive through an ATM.

Americans are experts at driving through things. There are even drive-through gas stations. In America, you can fill up your huge tank without having to go inside the service station—you just slide a credit card through the slot on the pump and when you're done, you can race off. At least until you hit the first red light.

Roads are generally wide enough to serve as emergency landing for distressed jumbo jets, yet all that concrete is deceptive: Many lanes are for turning only, which means you have to sit through— you guessed it—more red lights. By the time it's your turn to go, you've forgotten why you wanted to turn in the first place.

Maybe it was for fast food: there are approximately 160,000 fast food restaurants in the US, where of course the term "fast food" means you drive through a dedicated lane where you interact with three different fast food workers and 30 minutes later you finally receive your order at the last window.

Yet supermarkets, surprisingly, don't sell the variety of ready meals that they do in the UK. But they make up for it by the wide variety of food available right at the till. By the time you've finished shopping in a Super Sized Wal-Mart you're so famished you reach for one of the candy bars conveniently located by the check-out. Some Raisinets ought to make the drive home easier—surely this is what they mean by fruited plain!

Oh, America, you are indeed beautiful, despite your quirks. If only you'd embraced roundabouts the way you embraced the drive-through. Then I could get to Target much faster.

CHAPTER TEN

Weather

They say the weather in Britain is bad. They are right. Except when they're not, and those few days each summer when the weather is perfect are worth all the rain. Really.

April 22, 2006

April Is Not Always Cruel, But My Poetry Is

"Where should I dig now?"

IT'S A GORGEOUS DAY here, the first one this year. Temperature near 70F and not a cloud in sight.

It's days like today that make me wish I could write poetry, odes to Mother Earth in honor of her special day.

If I could, I'd write about the swan I saw flying toward Heathrow this morning, slowly gliding toward the runways. She knew she was much more glorious than the silver 767s lined up to migrate across the Atlantic. As she slid through the air currents, the Boeing birds took off awkwardly ahead of her, envying her grace, no doubt.

I'd write haiku about the spring that finally came, all at once, with fields of daffodils growing wild as dandelions. Bluebells lie in wait to replace them. Warm earth basks in sun.

I'd write a limerick about my dog, helping me dig in the mucky mud that is my flower bed. There once was a mutt from South Bucks...who dug and dug in some muck...her mom said "dig over here" and so she did. The dab of dirt looked cute between her eyes.

But I can't write poetry, despite being born in the middle of Poetry Month, so this will have to do:

"What instruments we have agree; it was a gorgeous day."

January 9, 2007

Weather Report

When one tugs at a single thing in nature, he finds it attached to the rest of the world. —John Muir

2006 WAS THE HOTTEST YEAR ever for the U.K. 2007 promises to be hotter.

Remember the drought we had last summer? Now we're having rain almost every day, for the last month or so. I can count on one hand the days I've seen the sun. It tried to put in an appearance yesterday, but by the time I was ready to go for a walk it was raining.

It's not a serious downpour kind of rain; instead it's drizzly and anemic.

Today we have gales of 60 mph. There's a piece of cardboard over our fireplace, to keep out the drafts, or rather the draughts. During windy weather, noises come from the fireplace that sound exactly like a crackling fire. I like that. It's sort of a green alternative to burning a fire.

We also have a stream in our back garden that normally is dry. (In the South, we'd call this a ditch, but Brits are more optimistic.) For the last month it's been a raging torrent. I like listening to it. Makes me think I live near a waterfall.

Plus it drowns out the sounds of the nearby M25.

Come to think of it, it's all those noisy cars on the M25 that are responsible for this climate mess we're in.

February 5, 2009

This Class Is Not For Wimps!

SNOW, SLEET, RAIN AND FOG...I ran into all those on my drive to class this morning. I take continuing ed classes at Oxford once a week, which is normally about a 45 minute drive, or an hour with traffic. Today, with a few inches of snow already fallen, there was little traffic, and when I walked into class, there were only six of us there—out of twenty-five. We spent some time congratulating each other for our determination and grit—and making fun of those who didn't make it.

I'm from Wisconsin, I scoffed. This is nuthin!

Sometimes it's fun being the only American in the class.

One thing we talked about in class was whether historical fiction can be relied on for an accurate picture of life during that time. I took the negative view, explaining that a novelist, even a 19th century novelist, will sanitize and condense, achieving verisimilitude rather than an actual accounting of fact. Not that Dickens' London was inaccurate, necessarily, but Dickens' goal was to write a readable novel, not create a historical record of his times.

Strangely, one of the women in class disagreed. "What about *Gone With the Wind?*" she asked. "I've never been to the American South but surely it's a realistic depiction."

I wish I could say I remembered all those times I've been embarrassed in class by my own ignorance and that I cut the poor woman some slack, but I laughed out loud. Guffawed quite rudely, I'm ashamed to say.

Gone With the Wind is nothing like the American South during the Civil War, I told her, and in fact, Margaret Mitchell didn't even live during the Civil War—she wrote the novel in the 1930s.

I bet that woman wished I'd stayed home that day.

December 2, 2010

A Not So Modest Proposal

ONCE AGAIN, MUCH of the UK has come screeching to a halt due to what, in any other advanced country, would be a relatively low-impact snowstorm. Much of the southeast, East Anglia, and the northeast got a few inches of snow, some places as much as 15 centimeters yesterday, with more having dropped last night.

Gatwick Airport will be closed for another day. The M20 is closed to Folkestone, diverting to the A20. Thousands of schools are closed, some for a fourth day, which means parents are forced to stay home from work to look after their children. So offices, shops, and other businesses are operating at diminished capacity.

And don't think public transportation will save you—trains have ceased operations in some parts of the country, and the airwaves were full of stories last night about stranded commuters.

I've lived in places in the US which get about as much snow as the UK. Ohio is a good example. I remember once driving through Ohio to Pennsylvania, just as a snowstorm was expected to hit. We admired the legions of snow plows poised in the median of the interstate, armed for battle with overflowing salt dispensers and sword-like plows pointed toward the ground. (In fact, I think we waxed poetical about them, odes which are, thankfully, long since lost.)

Such a sight doesn't happen here. Oh, they grit the roads, with a mixture of sand and salt. But I've never seen a proper plow, with a giant shovel in front for shoveling away the snow. And from the hundreds of traffic cameras fixed on the motorways, you can easily see that that's the problem: too much snow in the roads, despite the grit. (There is no shortage of traffic cameras on UK roads. Which says something about priorities that should be saved for another rant.)

What they need here is proper snow removal equipment.

Which leads to my proposal: The UK should buy snow plows from the United States. Thousands of them.

This will help the trade imbalance in the US, a vital step toward full economic recovery, as well as provide a stimulus for the economy. Since trained snow plow operators would be needed, unemployment would be eased as well. Meanwhile, here in the UK, productivity would increase as millions of workers could continue to show up for work. Travelers, like me, would carry on with their travel plans and continue to stimulate the economy of Europe.

It's a win-win proposition, no?

I've even done the research for you. The TowPlow has received high compliments from the state of Missouri, which uses them to clear their motorways. You can go to VikingCives.com to buy one. Or a few thousand.

Although you'll probably have to wait until the civil servants are able to return to work.

Failing this, perhaps they could recondition the up-for-sale aircraft carrier *HMS Invincible* (ha!) into much needed snow plows.

December 17, 2011

My White Christmas Nightmare

FOR THE LAST WEEK, I've been casting worried glances at the weather reports. My iPad has a neat weather app that predicts the weather five days out for any city in the world, including major airports. I was honed in to Heathrow on Friday, when Daughter Number One was scheduled to arrive.

You see, last year she was due to land right at the very moment snow was blanketing the runways at Heathrow. Watching her flight on radar, I saw it circle the airport several times, a typical maneuver as planes stack up. The snow here (twenty minutes from Heathrow) had stopped, so when the flight disappeared off radar I figured it had landed.

No, Flight 78 had headed in the opposite direction, to Charles de Gaulle in Paris. The plane landed safely (the French clear their runways très vite), disgorged its passengers, and there it stayed, well, until it was redirected to Miami a day later.

The passengers weren't so lucky. Holiday travelers found themselves stranded in Paris with no way to reschedule a flight to Heathrow, which remained essentially closed for days. This was Saturday; by Monday afternoon, we realized there was no way Heathrow (and its operator, BAA) could figure out how to remove five inches of snow from their runways (despite my many tweets offering to help). My husband announced he was driving to Paris and as he left, I booked his passage through Eurotunnel.

Long (and frustrating) story short, Daughter Number One (and two fellow passengers she met while stranded) finally were repatriated early in the morning of the Winter Solstice. (We of course immediately left for Stonehenge, to pay homage to the sun in hopes it would never abandon us again.)

So flash forward to this year: When the forecast predicted snow and sleet for Friday morning, I was concerned. No, that's too mild a word. All the anger and frustration I'd felt a year ago rose to the surface. For the last two years, we've had snow in December. Not that unusual, not even here in balmy England. Yet the locals reacted as if the Germans had launched a modern Blitz. Schools were cancelled, minor roads were impassable, sidewalks remained icy and dangerous for a week. Urban myths warned people not to clear their pavement (sidewalk): if you do, and someone slipped, you'd be liable to be sued, since you actually interfered with Mother Nature.

Well, I don't know about Mother Nature, but this mother was pissed. I wanted to scream at my lazy neighbors who didn't bother clearing their sidewalks, hurl insults at the idiots from BAA who appeared on the Beeb defending themselves for not knowing how to clear a few inches of snow from the busiest runway in the world.

I started the 2010 holidays off in a bad mood. So I didn't want to repeat that this year. When we saw huge fat snowflakes falling around nine a.m., I panicked. But the travel gods were on our side this year: the snow stopped, never accumulating, and Daughter's plane, delayed out of Dallas, landed an hour late. By the time we picked her up at Heathrow, the sun was shining and Mother Nature, I swear to god, was smiling.

Happy holidays. I'll try not to hit you if you wish for a white Christmas. Really. I'm over that.

May 9, 2012

Weather, Or Not

> *"It was very wet, we were just driving ... and looked up and realised one part of the sky was moving in one direction and another in the opposite direction. I thought 'That looks like a tornado!'"* —*quote from YouTube video of a "tornado" in England.*

WE'VE HAD A SPECTACULAR run of bad weather here in not-so-jolly England. The wettest April ever is, apparently, being followed by the wettest and coldest May ever. Last weekend saw temperatures lower than those on Christmas (Saturday's high here was 46F) and this weekend is predicted to be only slightly warmer. The sun did pop out for an hour or so yesterday afternoon, but I'm pretty sure that's the only time he showed his bright face since May Day.

And there's no end in sight, according *The Telegraph*. I've discovered that when it comes to weather news, *The Telegraph* is the place to go. *The Guardian* and *The Independent* can't seem to be bothered, unless they can tie the bad weather to the Tories in some way, while the BBC website has sparse content compared to the national newspapers.

But for some reason, the conservative *Telegraph* seems to be as preoccupied by the weather as I am. Perhaps that's because many of their readers live in the countryside and are old, and everyone knows old people have nothing more to talk about than the weather.

Since I live in the countryside, sort of, and am old, sort of, I've been spending an inordinate amount of time gazing at the Met Office radar page, wondering just when and where the big blue blobs will strike.

A few weeks ago I planted grass seed. Our lawn is looking really straggly, what with the drought we're having—that's right, a drought! That's one of those words that doesn't quite mean the same thing here as it does in America. Last year had about 5 inches off the normal yearly rainfall of 32 inches (as near as I can tell, having made rough conversions from mm to inches in my head). Which still gives us about three times the yearly average rainfall of New Mexico. Yet we're in the midst of a two-year drought and are now, despite record rainfall in April, living under a hosepipe ban.

It's mindboggling. I wish I knew exactly why we're having so much rain, but when I read stories like the one in *The Telegraph*, all I see is that the "unsettled" weather will continue.

Where's the low pressure? How many millibars? Any high pressure in sight? And what are the chances, in percentages, that I'll see rain between 2 and 3 pm? In other words, where's the science and specificity we Americans are used to in our forecasts? Are all the meteorologists busy tweeting for @MetOffice?

And what's this about a tornado in Oxfordshire, filmed by a couple in their car as they "pretty much drove right through it"?

Forecasters believe the tornado was caused by a "supercell" storm — a weather phenomenon more common to the US than the UK — in which the air in the storm spins.

"In which the air in the storm spins." That's the *Guardian*, talking to its readers as if they're three-year-olds.

I don't think the word "tornado" means what you think it means, either. You don't drive through the "spinning air" of a tornado; you get the hell out of the way, and if you don't have a storm cellar, you start praying, regardless of the fact you're a *Guardian*-reading heathen.

But I must confess, I'm to blame for the unsettled wet weather we've had. You see, I had the audacity to order new garden furniture in April. It's still sitting in my garage, in boxes, waiting for summer, since spring, apparently, is skipping 2012.

On the other hand, my grass seed is coming along quite nicely, despite the hosepipe ban. If only I could figure out how to wash my muddy wellies without a hosepipe—because I'm sure my nosy neighbour would rat me out if I pulled out my watering hose, even for a few minutes.

I suppose I could tell them I'm American, and the word "hosepipe" doesn't mean the same thing in my language.

June 14, 2012

Our Long, National Drought Continues

THE OTHER DAY I drove through the pouring drought to Folkstone, my windshield wipers furiously flinging the water away so that I could get to the train on time. And when we came home hours later, we drove back through the drought-parched jungle of southern England while more drought clouds dripped sprinkles on us, taunting us with our inability to use a hosepipe.

See how I've adjusted my language to the dialect of my adopted country? I know now that a "drought" is really a fancy British word for "malingering showers." And a hosepipe ban, a necessary component of a drought, is more of that wry British humor Americans seem incapable of understanding.

We spent Tuesday in France, where they seem to be having a drought on, too. The fields between Calais and Boulogne-sur-Mer were verdant and green, and the whole time we were in the Nausicaa aquarium the cold rain poured outside. Even the fish were glad to be indoors on such a day.

Some water companies lifted the hosepipe ban yesterday, in a fun little twist on irony. Yet my water company is determined to stick to the script. No hosepipe relief for its customers, no sirree! We'll suffer through this drought thingy, come hell or high water!

High water it is, then.

Americans watching our damp Jubilee celebrations were probably wondering why on earth England scheduled a Jubilee during a "drought." (Scare-quotes necessary to clue in you Yanks to the ironic use of that word.) Since the Jubilee celebration seemed entirely arbitrary, why not schedule them whenever they could do some good, tempting the gods to rain on our parade—literally—and ease dry conditions much more effectively than cloud seeding?

We could ease any future recession at the same time, by increasing sales of bunting.

Bunting and brollies! We'll have a right jolly olde time! (On the other hand, our rain butts will sit swollen and useless, alongside our limp hosepipes. C'est la vie!)

Long live the Queen! May she reign—or is that rain?—indefinitely. Or at least until we get some proper weather.

July 4, 2012

Summertime Blues

"WHY AM I NOT IN FRANCE RIGHT NOW?" demands my pathetic lavender.

NO, I'M NOT ONE of those people who think that plants have feelings, but the other day when I examined my sad lavender plant, I thought I heard a reproachful voice beseeching me to send it to France, where the climate is more suited to lavender than this godforsaken country.

Lavender doesn't like rain. Lavender doesn't like cold. Lavender doesn't like day after cloudy day of the nuclear winter-like conditions known as "summertime" that is England in 2012.

It's official: June was the dullest month since 1909. And the coldest in 20 years. And the wettest, well, since Queen Vic could sit on the throne without risk of it breaking.

All these broken records, which is exactly what I sound like these days, complaining about yet another day of miserable weather. I've decided my least favorite word is "overcast." Even when it's not outright raining, the sun is hiding behind a layer of clouds. The temperature rarely reaches 20C, or gets out of the mid-60s for those of a Fahrenheit mind.

It's churlish to complain, when my fellow Americans are roasting, toasting, and fanning themselves with whatever's handy since they lost electricity due to freak storms that knocked out power lines. I feel bad for them, I really do, but I still wish they'd quit posting photos on Facebook of themselves wearing shorts and eating outside. My new garden furniture has been covered with green plastic covers ever since we put it outdoors. After having it in the garage for weeks, we finally got it out for a week of warm sunny weather in May. Mother Nature's a tease.

We've hardly seen a day of sun since the first of June. We should be firing up barbecues, donning shorts and swimwear, and complaining about the horrid heat by now, the Fourth of July.

I don't see any relief in sight. The Met Office has just issued a weather alert for much of England over the next few days. Since the ground is saturated, we're to be on the lookout for flash floods.

However, if we do get a flash flood and our garage floods, we won't be able to wash it out with our hosepipe. Because we're still under a hosepipe ban. Because of the drought.

It's a sign of how the weather has got me down that I don't even find that irony funny anymore.

November 26, 2012

"I Won't Stop the Rain By Complaining"? Watch Me Try.

I DON'T KNOW WHAT B.J. Thomas was smoking when he wrote that song, but I want some.

I swore I was not going to blog about the weather again but, the RAIN! The rain WON'T STOP!

Southern England is flooding again, and what ground is not flooded is saturated with water. Walking next to the streets here (where there are no pavements, i.e. sidewalks) means squishing along, hoping when the shoe manufacturer claimed your shoes were "waterproof" they really had tested them in the proving grounds of England after 40 days of rain.

Forty days? Or thirty-nine? Who's counting?

Our summer of showers turned into a fall of alternating drizzle and downpours, and I expect a winter of sleet and snow is on its way. I'm trying not to obsess too much, but chains have been ordered for our car and I've sharpened the snow shovel. Just in case.

I hear there's a drought still going on in the US. The problem is that we got America's share of precipitation. Perhaps the two countries should consider a treaty, a precipitation exchange.

I swear to God I'm going to slit my wrist—with my snow shovel—if this doesn't stop soon.

Oh yes, "the blues they send to meet me" may just defeat me, if these damn raindrops don't stop fallin' on my head.

"It won't be long till happiness steps up to greet me." I call bullshit. Or else Jamaican High Grade.

April 12, 2013

Get Thee From Me, Garden Catalogs!

The "wicked plot" with which I tempted Fate last Spring.

As I SIT HERE TYPING, it is once again raining. The weather experts promise brighter weather ahead this weekend, after condemning us to a miserable March and equally miserly first two weeks of April.

Last year about this time I inadvertently brought the wrath of the weather gods upon all of Britain: I bought garden furniture. I also bought flowers and plants and grass seeds. I planned to have a spectacular garden, which I'd enjoy from my new Lutyens bench, next to the chiminea on cool evenings.

What was I thinking, tempting Fate with such abandon?

For the past several years, our plans had been in flux: we assumed we'd be moving back to the US each of the previous few summers, so planting anything in the garden didn't seem worth it, nor did I see any reason to replace my old metal patio table with a new one.

But last year we knew we'd be staying on, at least through another year. So I indulged. But buying patio furniture is apparently one of the Seven Deadly Sins, and in this case, it resulted in Seven Deadly Months of rain and slugs. It's as if my capriciousness reached into the atmosphere and bent the jet stream, causing untold misery to millions.

I'm pretty much all powerful like that.

The Lord hateth a "heart that devises wicked plots," the Proverbs claim. Buying garden furniture and annuals and potting soil is surely more wicked than *Fifty Shades of Grey*, which I also suspect had something to do with last summer's weather.

It's about time for the garden catalogs to arrive. I shall condemn them immediately to the recycle bin. I'm getting emails with tempting discounts from the many garden centres I signed up for last year, and I quickly send them to cyber hell. I haven't even uncovered my Lutyens bench; that would be like leaving home without an umbrella.

Our cold spring has meant the bluebells will likely be late this year. I saw signs of them in Hedgerley on Easter Sunday, the coldest Easter on record. The puny green shoots shivered in the mud, while about them daffodils regretted ever coming above ground.

Cold weather in January is one thing; cold temperatures in April are quite another. It didn't help that our boiler went out last Thursday. It took five days for the replacement to be installed, five days during which we shivered, most of the house shut off so we could contain the heat from the two space heaters the plumber loaned us.

It's been great to have heat again these last few days (and more efficient heat at that!). But now I'd really like some of that heat outdoors. I'd like to take a walk without gloves and a scarf. I'd like to sit next to my chiminea and enjoy a piña colada...okay, I'm getting carried away.

Even thinking of a piña colada could bend the jet stream.

If it hits 20C as predicted on Sunday, you can bet I'll celebrate. But I swear, as God is my witness, I will never buy garden furniture again.

June 17, 2013

Weather Whinging

I WAS ALL SET to write about the weather this morning, and then I read that it might get to 30° (86F) this week. (Caveat: "might" is the operative word. Other models suggest that it will only get to 26°, and that's in the Midlands, one spot in England, while the rest of the country will have temperatures in the lower twenties.) So, with the prospect of actual summer weather on its way, I can't exactly succumb to another round of whinging about the weather, can I?

Oh, watch me. It's been unseasonably cold all spring, and unseasonably cool for the past month. My car thermometer reads "59" every time I look at it, leading me to believe it's stuck in the fifties (Fahrenheit—my car speaks American). I'm really sick and tired of wearing several layers just to walk the dog.

I remember when I moved here and the first summer we had several days with highs in the fifties. I thought that was unusual, but my hairdresser told me it was perfectly normal. I dismissed that as British pessimism, but she was right. Summers here can have lovely spells, which is why I tend not to go anywhere during the summer months, determined as I am to eek out every morsel of rare good weather, but these spells are interspersed with weeks of damp, cold, misery.

This chill, this cold damp, is not what I think of when I think "summer." I grew up in the American South, where a cold blast of air conditioning was a welcome thing, where afternoons were for staying indoors and keeping cool anyway you could.

Summers are supposed to be hot. Summers are for wearing shorts and sundresses. These days, when I see someone wearing shorts and sleeveless tops, I feel a stab of jealousy. And beach photos turn me positively green: do you people in warm climates know how lucky you are? (Wisconsin and Minnesota, I'm including you in this.)

I'm starting to really hate Floridians, with their beach parties and bikinis and shimmery tans. I see you all up on Facebook, lounging next to your pools, bobbing your babies in their cute little blowup duckies, wearing sunshades the size of melons. I want a piece of that—the melon, too. It just doesn't get hot enough here for good watermelon.

If it does hit 30 on Wednesday—86; that sounds warmer—I'll ransack my drawers looking for the one pair of denim shorts I own, and throw them on while I take the dog for a walk in the hottest part of the day. I'll have to slather on sunscreen, since my limbs haven't been touched by the sun in at least three years. On the other hand, if it's only 23°, I'll engage in more whinging, since I've learned to do that really well.

CHAPTER ELEVEN

Drawing a Line Under It

They call it a "special relationship," that closeness that exists between America and Britain. Sometimes it's a love-hate relationship for me, but more often, it's just love.

July 28, 2012

England's Green and Pleasant Land

My, what a difference an opening ceremony makes.

SEVEN YEARS AGO, when the Olympic Committee announced London as the location of the 2012 Olympics, I yawned. Great, but I wouldn't be around to see it. I'd be back in the United States, where I belonged. It would be painful to watch, I figured, seeing the familiar scenes, hearing the familiar accents, spotting the familiar landmarks.

But a funny thing happened to our plans. They changed. And changed again. And with my constantly changing plans, my love for England waxed and waned. Familiarity breeds contempt, they say, but even more, the thought of parting breeds careful condescension.

When our five years were up, I decided it would be helpful if I didn't like living here anymore. So I began finding things to dislike about England and her people. Too inept, I decided, when Heathrow closed for five days after receiving five inches of snow. (That was an easy one.) Too anti-American, I argued, after reading yet another list of "most hated Americanisms." Not innovative enough, not warm enough, not flexible enough—and all the nonsense about the Olympic committee's determination to protect their sponsors at the expense of our crisp packets played right into that, I must say.

I went on like that for two or three years, expecting to leave here with a not-too-heavy heart, any month now. Twice we came close to moving to the States, and twice our plans were cancelled at virtually the last minute.

And now, in the summer of 2012, I've found out there is no plan to move, not in the near future. We are here for a while yet.

But my love for England had not waxed at all this summer. Until a week or so ago, we were trapped by a perverse jet stream, locked in a monochrome weather pattern of non-stop rain and clouds. My mood was grim. This god-forsaken land, no longer green but 50 shades of grey, no longer pleasant but muddy and damp, could no more enchant me than that silly Olympic mascot.

But the jet stream turned. The countenance divine shone forth on these clouded hills, as William Blake would say. Or as I would say, the sun came out, in all its 30C glory.

Summer in England was always my favorite season.

And so last night, I watched the opening ceremony of the Olympics, my windows and doors wide open to let the evening breeze in, BBC on the telly, and my Twitter app open on my phone, ready to share my cynicism with the rest of the viewing world.

They had me at the source of the Thames.

I remember searching, once, for the source of the great River Thames, the first spring I lived here. With a couple of friends, I puttered around in my little red car, my chariot of fire, through Gloucestershire—the Shire, crossing footpaths and wandering around lush fields. We never found it, but we all fell in love with this green and pleasant land.

Last night's ceremony moved me, with all its not-at-all understated special effects, its improbable helo landing of the Queen—as in Her Majesty—and its reminder of that other Queen, those other pop legends. Its inclusiveness, its innovativeness, its lack of timidity, were a timely reminder of what Great Britain, this "peculiar and contrary" country means to me, if not to the world.

I won't go on: there are reviews aplenty. Director Danny Boyle explains it best in his statement on the ceremony's purpose, beginning with a quote from another great Englishman, William Shakespeare: "Be not afeard: the isle is full of noises."

"But we hope, too, that through all the noise and excitement you'll glimpse a single golden thread of purpose—the idea of Jerusalem—of the better world, the world of real freedom and true equality, a world that can be built through the prosperity of industry, through the caring nation that built the welfare state, through the joyous energy of popular culture, through the dream of universal communication. A belief that we can build Jerusalem. And that it will be for everyone."

Including me, it seems.

March 1, 2014

A Return to Distant Shores

AT SOME POINT, probably this summer, a moving van will show up on my cul-de-sac. A lorry, I've learned to call them. Its purpose will be to load up ten years of my life and send it packing, back to my homeland.

But not the land of my heart.

America isn't the same place it was when I left it. And I am not the same person. We'll have some adjusting to do; as much, I imagine, as when I moved here ten years ago.

"Here" will no longer be *here*, and I'll read this and weep, most likely, for those days I spent sorting out my life on the edge of the English countryside.

I'll weep for the footpaths, the stiles, the kissing gates. I'll weep for the castles, the crowns, the kingdom that my ancestors left, probably because they wanted larger parking spaces.

I hope it's a dreary day. I hope the rain clouds hover overhead, taunting me with their unremitting presence. I hope the jet stream turns into a slinky with enough kinks to keep the weather miserable for the two weeks it will take to fully take my leave of these shores.

But if only it were merely the weather! There's more, so much more, to compensate for a winter's worth of rain, the mildew of a damp spring.

Just one walk along the Thames can erase a fortnight of autumnal fog.

And the museums and theatres in London are the perfect place to spend a rainy afternoon.

The teasing emails will fill my inbox, from the National Theatre, English Heritage, the British Museum. From my walking buddies, with news of another Wednesday hike in the Chilterns. From the continuing ed department at Oxford, with the next term's offerings.

I can unsubscribe from emails but not from my memories.

I've never lived in one place for a decade, save that tract home in the suburbs where I spent twelve years of my childhood. We suffered grief in this house—the deaths of our parents and our beloved dog, our daughters both leaving the proverbial nest for good. There was joy, too: our daughters' successes, news of my publishing contract, an election in America that made us glow with pride.

This is Home. There was an indefinable feeling of rightness I felt when I came here and saw lush gardens and an abundance of green, green grass. It felt, inexplicably, like I'd come home, after long years in an alien Midwest, and in the dry heat of the Southwest. Some vestige of my ancestry, perhaps. A strand of DNA encoded with the geography of Southern England as well as instructions for ginger hair and pale skin.

Eventually, I'll relearn driving skills I lost when I took to roundabouts like a guppy to a slippery stream. I'll adjust to the odd way Americans have of speaking what's on their mind, loudly and with fervor. I'll imitate the long vowels in "tomato" and have a yard instead of a garden.

A transplant, once again.

Reading through these chapters, ten years of my life condensed into a couple hundred pages, it seems as if I've had a love-hate relationship with England and the English people. The truth is, it's been a lopsided relationship: about 80% love, 20% hate, and most of that can be attributed to the operators of Heathrow in December, 2010.

Defra: The Department for Environment, Food and Rural Affairs. Responsible for allowing dogs and cats into England.

Dodgy: In America the word "sketchy" about covers it.

Dual carriageway: A divided highway.

Dust bin: A euphemism for rubbish bin, or as we'd call it in the US, garbage can.

Engineer: A technician. Note that an engineer in Britain is not the highly trained professional (requiring at least a four-year college degree) that the word refers to in the US. The man who repairs your security alarm will call himself an "engineer," even though he's probably only had a six-month training course.

Estate agent: A real estate agent or property manager.

Estate car: A station wagon.

Flyover: An overpass on the roadway.

Fly-tipping: The practice of illegally dumping your rubbish on the side of the road or in other unapproved places.

Footpath: One of thousands of paths, or trails, throughout the countryside. They are always open to the public even if the footpath crosses private property.

FTSE: (pronounced "footsie") The Financial Times Stock Exchange. It tracks stock indices on the London stock exchange, similar to the Dow Jones in the US.

Full-stop: A vague word for the punctuation called a "period" in the US.

Fun Fair: The local carnival-type fair that comes to every small town or village every few months, setting up in the Common or other open areas.

Garden: A more delightful way of saying "yard." (Note that a "yard" refers to a paved area usually found at a construction firm.) There may or may not be flowers in a garden, but it does not mean a place to grow vegetables.

Hamlet: A very small village, usually without a church or pub.

High street: Similar to "main street" in the US, a "high street" is where shops are located.

Holiday: A vacation, not necessarily occurring over a holiday period.

Identity parade: A picturesque way to refer to a police lineup. You won't usually find clowns in this type of parade.

Inverted comma/s: Quotation marks, either a single (used where Americans would use double quote marks) or double, used inside a passage set off within single quote marks. Confused?

Kitchen roll: Paper towels. Similarly, "toilet roll" refers to toilet paper.

Ladybird: The small red insect known as a ladybug in the US.

Lift: An elevator.

Loft: The attic.

Lorry: A large truck, often called an "18 wheeler" in the US. Note: never used to refer to a pick-up truck.

Mains: Refers to the power that comes out of your wall. The mains can be shut off separately at each switch plate. There is no exact equivalent in the US.

Maths: Mathematics (which actually makes more sense, since the root word has an "s" on the end).

Mothering Sunday: Mother's Day, only it occurs in March.

Motorway: Limited access highway. We'd call this an Interstate in the US. Also referred to as "M-roads" as they are always designated M1, M2, etc. An A-road is a lesser road, though some are dual carriageways. B-roads are minor roads.

Nappy: Diaper.

Overtake: To pass someone on a road or highway. (Note that the passing lane is on the opposite side and is used strictly for overtaking, never for cruising along as in the US.)

Pants: Underwear, i.e. panties. Do not call your "trousers" pants or you could get into trouble. Note: Pants can also mean rubbish, as in, "This book is pants!"

Pear shaped: A lovely expression that means something has gone quite wrong. Oh dear.

Public school: This word means quite the opposite to what it says. A "public school" is a very exclusive private school. What Americans think of as "public schools" are called "state schools" in Britain. There are also "private schools" which aren't quite so exclusive.

Pudding: A catch-all word meaning dessert, while "dessert" refers to something a bit more fancy, likely something French.

Push chair: A baby stroller, also called a "pram."

Quid: A pound (unit of money, not weight). Don't add an s for plural: Ten quid, not ten quids.

Radio 4, etc.: The BBC radio stations are named Radio 1-6. Radio 4 is the talk channel similar to, but better than, NPR.

Recovery: This refers to towing a disabled car from the roadside with a recovery vehicle, i.e. a tow truck.

Roadworks: Road construction is referred to as "roadworks" and there are special speed limits assigned (50 mph on the motorway).

Row: An argument. (Rhymes with "cow.")

Rubbish: A word that usually refers to garbage, but also can be a verb, meaning "to denigrate something, i.e. "He rubbished my reputation," or an adjective "my rubbish car won't start."

Sat nav: A GPS device for the car.

Services: Similar to a rest area in the US, but with services such a a petrol (gas) station, fast food restaurants, and bookshop Expect to find clean toilets (i.e., restrooms) at a motorw services.

Shipping Forecast: A weather forecast broadcast twice a day on BBC radio announcing the weather conditions in the northern Atlantic waters.

Single-track road: A one-lane road found in the countryside, with wider areas every few hundred yards where one car can pull over to let the other car pass.

Skip: A Dumpster. Often seen outside homes being renovated.

Slip road: The exit road on a motorway.

Solicitor: An attorney.

Strimmer: A weedwacker.

Surgery: This may be where your doctor dispenses advice (a doctor's office, in the US), but it may also be where your doctor operates on you. It may also be where your MP (Member of Parliament) has a local office where they listen to constituents' complaints.

The Archers: A long running radio drama on BBC's Radio 4.

Tin: A can, as in "tinned beans."

Toasty stand: A temporary setup, usually found at a fair or market, where grilled sandwiches called "toasties" are served.

Toff: A rather derogatory term for a member of the upper class.

Toilet: A public restroom. (Note that bathrooms are inside homes and contain an actual bath.) Also called W.C. for water closet.

Torch: A flashlight.

Washing up liquid: Dishwashing liquid.

Whilst: An old-fashioned way of saying "while."

Whinge: To complain or whine.

Yank: A word referring to Americans, or Yankees. No distinction is made for Americans from the Southern United States.

·b: A youth, typically one making trouble. The word's origins said to be "boy" spelt backwards.

ssing: A pedestrian crossing marked by wide white n the road. Cars must give way to pedestrians at every ossing. (Other pedestrian crossings are known as pelican crossings, toucan crossings, and puffin crossings. I am not making this up!)

Zed: The letter Z, as in "the A to zed," which refers to a popular map of London.

48797904R00132

Made in the USA
San Bernardino, CA
04 May 2017